SELF-WORKING
PAPER MAGIC
81 FOOLPROOF TRICKS

KARL FULVES

With 367 Illustrations by Joseph K. Schmidt

DOVER PUBLICATIONS, INC.
NEW YORK

Self-Working Paper Magic: 81 Foolproof Tricks is a new work, first published by Dover Publications, Inc., in 1985.

Library of Congress Cataloging in Publication Data

Fulves, Karl.
  Self-working paper magic.

  1. Tricks.   2. Paper work.   I. Title.
GV1559.F843   1985   793.5   84-21179
ISBN-13: 978-0-486-24847-9
ISBN-10: 0-486-24847-X

Manufactured in the United States by RR Donnelley
24847X12   2016
www.doverpublications.com

INTRODUCTION

Learn a few tricks with paper and you will be prepared to perform magic anytime. Paper magic has the advantage of being lightweight, inexpensive and portable. The tricks in this book pack flat, take up little space, yet are big in effect.

Will Blyth and Harry Houdini were among the first magicians to write books that dealt exclusively with paper magic. In the years since the publication of their books, the literature on paper magic has expanded dramatically. Today it is possible to perform a complete magic act with paper.

Numerous books on paper magic devote space to origami and paper cutting. Many people, myself included, have trouble following the directions for all but the simplest such tricks. Accordingly, although this book contains tricks in which paper is folded and cut, the tricks have been chosen for ease in handling and simplicity of method.

The material includes some tricks with single sheets of paper, but the definition of paper magic has been expanded to include everything from paper cups to paper bags and paperback books. There is even a trick with the book you are now reading.

For their generous assistance I would like to thank Robert E. Neale, Sam Schwartz, Howard Wurst, Martin Gardner, Tony Bartolotta, Sam Randlett and Joseph K. Schmidt.

CONTENTS

MAGIC WITH PAPER

Among the varied tricks with paper in this chapter are a routine in which a newspaper vanishes and a psychic routine in which two paper rings magically link.

Although some of the tricks require preparation, they are easy to perform. A puzzling routine such as "The Magic Mailbox" (No. 4) works best as a close-up trick, whereas "Japanese Checkers" (No. 1) can be done as a showy stage effect. In all cases the inexpensive props may be given away as souvenirs when the tricks are over.

1 JAPANESE CHECKERS

The magician shows a checkerboard made from a sheet of paper. He cuts it up into 12 squares which he drops into a paper bag and mixes. He says that he once met a gambler who would bet he could reach into the bag and remove all 12 squares in less than a second.

The magician reaches into the bag and instantly removes all 12 squares. The trick is easy because they're all connected. There are no gimmicks or switches. Only one sheet of paper is used.

METHOD: This trick is based on a paper-cutting routine devised by the Japanese magician Shigeo Takagi. All that is required is a sheet of blank paper. Mark it off into squares as indicated in Figure 1, and color them in two colors. Mark corners A and B so you can follow the method used to cut the paper. Once you understand the handling it will not be necessary to mark the paper. The handling follows a simple pattern.

Fold the paper in half across the middle, Figure 2. Then cut along the crease from the bottom to a point about ½" from the top, Figure 3.

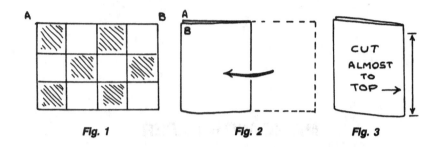

Fig. 1   **Fig. 2**   **Fig. 3**

Give the paper a 180° turn to the position shown in Figure 4. Fold along the dotted line, bringing the right side over onto the left side. The result is shown in Figure 5. Cut along the crease from the bottom up to a point about ½" from the top as shown in Figure 5.

The upper third of the paper is now folded down in front, Figure 6. The lower third is folded up in back, Figure 7.

Give the paper a 90° turn clockwise to the position of Figure 8. Cut along the crease at the right side from the bottom up to a point about ½" from the top.

Give the packet a 180° turn, bringing it to the position of Figure 9. Cut along the crease from the bottom up to a position about ½" from the top as shown in Figure 9.

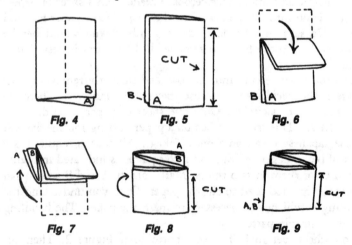

Fig. 4   **Fig. 5**   **Fig. 6**

Fig. 7   **Fig. 8**   **Fig. 9**

Throughout all of the folding and cutting it appears to the audience that you are cutting through the paper from bottom to top. They assume after the final cut that the paper has been divided into 12 separate squares. Hold corner A as you drop the cut paper into the paper bag. Shake the bag. Then pull out the paper, Figure 10, to show that all squares are connected.

Fig. 10

2 PROBABILITY ZERO

A packet of blank business cards is shown. On one side of each of nine of these cards the performer writes a number. After each number is written, the card is placed number-side down on the table. The performer explains that he is numbering the cards at random so that the spectators will get no clues as to which number is on what card. The cards are placed in a row on the table.

At the performer's request the spectator touches a card at random. On the back of this card the performer writes the number 1. The spectator touches a second card. The number 2 is written on the back of this card. The remainder of the cards are similarly numbered in the order indicated by the spectator. The last card, number 9, is left on the table. The other cards are dealt on top in reverse order, ending with card number 1 on top.

The spectator turns over the cards one at a time. It is found that the number on the back of each card correctly matches the number on the face. Thus, although the spectator touched cards at random, although he was in no way influenced in his selections and although he had no way of knowing the numbers written on the cards, he managed to choose the cards in numerical order.

METHOD: This ingenious trick was invented by Paul Curry. Use a packet of about 20 blank cards. Unruled 3"-by-5" file cards are available in office-supply stores. Cut ten cards in half, producing a packet of 20 cards, each measuring 2½" by 3".

Write the number 1 on both sides of one card. Write the number 2 on both sides of a second card. Proceed in this way up through the number 7. With the cards in order and the 7 card uppermost, drop the prenumbered group onto the remaining cards. On one side only of another card, write the number 8 and place it blank-side up on top of the number 7 card. This completes the preparation.

To perform the trick, remove the cards from your pocket. Hold them with the prepared group at the bottom. Show the top few cards and explain that you'll number some of the cards.

Hold the packet up so the audience can't see what you write. In the center of the first card write the number 9. The downstroke of the 9 should be curved so that if the card were turned around the 9 would become a 6. Don't press down too hard when you write; you don't want an impression to transfer through the card.

Without showing the writing, place this card number-side down on the table. Number the next eight cards in exactly the same way with a 9 on each card. Place the cards writing-side down alongside each other. There will be a row of nine cards on the table, each with the number 9 on its underside.

Request the spectator to touch any card. Place the touched card on top of the stack in your hand. Openly write the number 1 on the blank side of this card. Have the spectator touch a second card. Place this card on top of the stack. Write the number 2 on the blank upper surface of this card. Continue in this way until five cards have been numbered.

Let the spectator touch another card. No matter which card he touches, shake your head. Say, "You've been doing fine to this point, but I don't think that's the 6. Please try another card."

Whatever card the spectator touches, nod as if relieved and say, "That's better." Place this card on top of the stack and write a 6 on the upper surface. Openly turn over this card end for end and show that there is indeed a 6 on the other side. This is the reason why you drew the 9's with curved downstrokes. When turned upside down and viewed from the spectator's angle, any 9 becomes a 6.

After giving the spectator a glimpse of the 6, place the card on top of the number 5 card. Have the spectator choose one of the remaining cards. Place it on the packet blank-side up and write the number 7 on the upper surface.

Two cards remain on the table. Tell the spectator to be particularly careful in choosing the number 8. Whatever card he chooses, place it on top of the stack. Don't write on it just yet.

Hand him the pencil and tell him to write the number 9 on the remaining card. With the audience's attention misdirected to the spectator, you can secretly turn over the stack of cards. This can be done by dropping your hand to your side. As the spectator begins to write, quietly turn over the stack in your hand. At the completion of the turnover there will still be a blank surface showing on top of the stack, so all appears unchanged.

Take the pencil from the spectator and write the number 8 on the top card. Then deal this card onto the table alongside the number 9 card. Deal the remaining numbered cards onto the table, showing the 7, 6, 5, etc.

For the finish, step back and let the spectator turn over each card. He will be amazed to discover a perfect match.

You can have a blank set of cards in your pocket. When all attention is on the spectator, reach into your pocket, leave the packet in your hand inside your pocket and bring out the blank packet. Then the apparatus can be left with the audience.

This is in essence a trick in which the spectator correctly sorts out a packet of numbered cards which has been randomly mixed. A similar trick can be done with playing cards, as follows.

3 PROBABLE POKER

From an ordinary deck of playing cards the magician removes ten cards which make two pat hands. For those not familiar with draw-poker terminology, the magician explains that a pat hand is one, such as a straight (five cards of any suit in numerical sequence), a flush (any five cards of the same suit) or full house (three of a kind and a pair), in which all five cards are necessary to the hand.

The spectator mixes the ten cards and directs the magician in sorting them into two poker hands. When the hands are examined, it turns out that the spectator has sorted them into two pat hands.

METHOD: Beforehand, remove any 2–3–4–5–6–7–8–9–10. They should be in mixed suits. Arrange them in numerical order from the top down.

Next remove four jacks, four aces and two 6's. These cards can be in any random order.

Arrange the pack as follows. Place the face-down 2 through 10 in numerical order on top of the face-down deck. Turn the deck over so it is face up. Turn over the two face cards of the deck so they are face to face with the deck. Then place the ace-6-jack packet face down on these cards. The setup is shown in Figure 11.

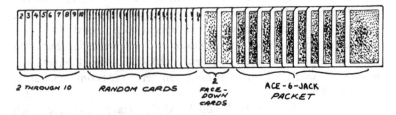

2 THROUGH 10   RANDOM CARDS   2 FACE-DOWN CARDS   ACE - 6 - JACK PACKET

Fig. 11

Hold the deck in your hand so the ace-6-jack packet is uppermost. The pack appears to be face down. Explain to the spectator that you want to test his poker I.Q. Deal off the top ten cards. Explain that these cards can be sorted in only one way to produce two pat hands at draw poker. Don't show the faces of the cards to the audience.

The spectator mixes the ten cards and deals them face down into a row on the table. Point out that no one, including yourself, knows the location of any card. Have the spectator choose five cards carefully. Take them from him one at a time and place them face down on top of the deck.

Then remark that of the five cards remaining he is to give you four, keeping one for himself as the hole card in his hand. Take the four designated cards from him one at a time. Place each of them face down on top of the deck.

One card remains face down on the table. Neither of you knows which card it is. Tell him to turn over this card. As attention is misdirected to this card, you can turn the deck over secretly. It is easiest to drop your hand to your side to perform the secret turnover.

Up to this point you did not know the identity of the card on the table. Its identity determines the way the trick is ended. If it's an ace or a 6, deal the top four cards of the deck onto it face down. If it's a jack, deal the top five cards to yourself. Then deal the next four cards face down onto the jack.

In either case have the spectator turn up each hand to show he correctly sorted the cards in the only possible way that would give both players a pat hand at draw poker.

4 THE MAGIC MAILBOX

This fascinating apparatus was invented by George Jarshaur. It is constructed from a single piece of paper. When completed it resembles a three-fold wallet. Many magical effects are possible with the Jarshaur wallet.

Start with a rectangular piece of paper measuring about 4" by 8". Place the paper on the table before you as in Figure 12. Fold the upper half down flush onto the lower half. The result is shown in Figure 13.

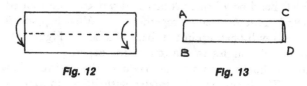

Fig. 12   **Fig. 13**

It's wise at this point to label the points A, B, C, D, as indicated in Figure 13. It will make later steps easier to follow if you're doing the fold for the first time, and you can check your progress at a glance by comparing the folded paper with the drawings.

Referring to Figure 14, bring corner C down so that CD is flush with BD. You will have formed a triangular piece on the right as depicted in Figure 15.

Now bring AB over to the right so that AB just meets the vertical side of the triangle, Figure 16. Crease the fold just formed, then bring AB back to the left. The result is shown in Figure 17. You have just created a centerline crease EF. (This is not the true center of the paper.)

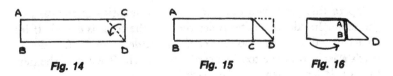

Fig. 14   Fig. 15   Fig. 16

Bring corner A down in the direction indicated by the arrow in Figure 17, so that AE is flush with EF. The result is as indicated in Figure 18.

Bring AB back to the original starting position. You have created a crease EG in the paper as shown in Figure 19.

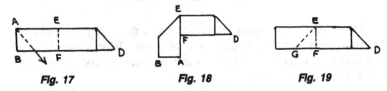

Fig. 17   Fig. 18   Fig. 19

Your right hand now grasps the paper just to the right of point F. Your left hand grasps the paper at corner A and your fingertips slip between the two layers at point A. The situation is as shown in Figure 20.

Your left hand now brings corner A down as if you wanted your thumbs and point A to come together at F. What happens is that the left panel will open up in the shape of a house, Figure 21. This house is at right angles to the rest of the paper.

Rotate the house around to the right to the position shown in Figure 22. The house actually rotates with EF as an axis.

Open the triangle at the right so the short right edge is vertical again. This is shown in Figure 23.

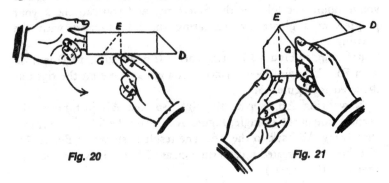

Fig. 20   Fig. 21

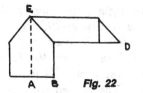

Fig. 22

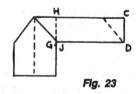

Fig. 23

In Figure 23 note the crease line HJ. This does not exist as yet but it is an extension of the line that starts at point B and moves straight up. The way to form HJ is to bring CD over to the left, Figure 24, with BG as an axis. Make the crease, then bring CD back to the right. The result will be the new crease HJ shown in Figure 23.

Bring corner C down so it is directly adjacent to corner B. The result is shown in Figure 25. After making the crease, bring corner C back to its original position. The result is the new crease HK, shown in Figure 26.

Your left hand grasps the left portion of the paper (the house on the left in Figure 26) up to the point labeled J. Your right hand now grips corner C, thumb on top, fingers between the folds, and brings point C down until it meets B. This is the same thing you did in Figure 21 and the result is the same. The right-side panel will open up in the shape of a house.

Swing this house to the left so it lies on top of the other house. The situation is shown in Figure 27. Point C is directly above B, and point D is directly above A.

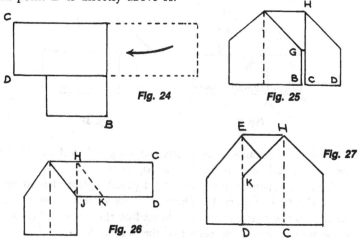

Fig. 24

Fig. 25

Fig. 26

Fig. 27

Referring to Figure 28, fold the right panel, shown shaded, around to the back. Then, referring to Figure 29, fold the left panel, shown shaded in Figure 29, around in back.

The situation now is as indicated in Figure 30. Open the construction by swinging the uppermost panel CD to the right, then the inner panel AB to the left. The opened structure looks like Figure 31. This completes the construction.

To illustrate the "Magic Mailbox" theme, in space AB write "Moscow." In space AC write "Boston." In space CD write "London." Then close up the structure by swinging AB to the center, then CD to the center. You are back to Figure 30.

Turn the entire apparatus over side for side (left to right). The apparatus will appear identical to Figure 30. Open it by swinging the upper panel to the right, then the next panel to the left. Then label the blank panel as indicated in Figure 32.

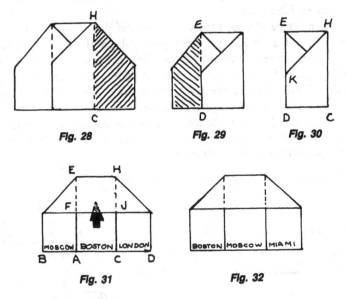

Fig. 28   Fig. 29   Fig. 30

Fig. 31   Fig. 32

Close the apparatus by swinging the left panel to the right, then the right panel over to the left on top of all.

Turn the apparatus over, secretly if possible, from left to right. You are back to Figure 30. Open it. Place a piece of paper under the flap in the center panel as indicated by the arrow in Figure 31. Make sure it lies in the center of the various folds.

Remark that the paper represents an airmail letter. You can even use an airmail stamp if one is handy. Ask the spectator if he wants the letter delivered to Moscow or London. When he names a city, fold the panel bearing that name over first. Then fold the other panel over on top of it.

Turn over the apparatus side for side (left to right). Open it and you will find the card still in the center, but the name in the center panel has magically changed to that of the city of the spectator's choice.

5 X-IT

The spectator holds a cardboard square behind his back and draws an X anywhere on it. He turns the cardboard over, writing-side down. The cardboard is given to the magician behind his back.

The magician displays a needle that has been threaded with a bright piece of ribbon. He places it behind his back and instantly pushes the needle into the exact center of the X.

Needle, thread and cardboard may be left with the spectator at the finish.

METHOD: Behind your back, concealed under your jacket, is a duplicate piece of cardboard which has an X on it. A duplicate threaded needle has been pushed into the center of the X. With this prior preparation done, the handling is as follows.

Hand the spectator a blank square of cardboard and a pen. Have him put the cardboard behind his back and draw a large X on it with the pen. He then turns the cardboard writing-side down and gives it to you behind your back. The spectator never sees the X he drew, so he is not aware later that his cardboard was switched.

Hand him a needle with a large eye and a piece of brightly colored ribbon. Have him thread the ribbon. While attention is on him, place his piece of cardboard under your belt in back. Secretly remove the duplicate cardboard and hold it behind your back.

Take the threaded needle from the spectator with your free hand. Place it behind your back. Immediately gather the ribbon into a small bundle. Ribbon and needle are tucked into a rear pocket or under the belt.

Bring out the duplicate cardboard already threaded. Show that you threaded the needle through the center of the X.

The trick can be done without the switch. You use only one cardboard, one needle and one piece of ribbon. The cardboard can be initialed by the spectator. There are no gimmicks and it is not necessary to glimpse the cardboard secretly. You can even be blindfolded.

The handling is this. Give the spectator a square of cardboard and a thick black crayon. While you turn your back, have him draw a small circle anywhere on the cardboard. He then turns the cardboard writing-side down and gives it to you behind your back.

Hand him the needle and ribbon. Have him thread the ribbon through the eye of the needle. While he does this, run your fingertips lightly over the cardboard. Since the O is drawn with crayon, it is drawn with wax. It is easy to find the location of the O on the cardboard by sense of touch.

Take the threaded needle from the spectator, place it behind your back and push it into the O.

6 CATCHING THE NEWS

The magician places a wadded piece of newspaper on his right arm, Figure 33. He snaps his forearm downward and catches the paper in his hand, Figure 34. The stunt is repeated, but this time the paper vanishes. It is found in his pocket. Only one piece of paper is used.

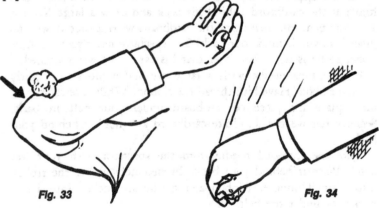

Fig. 33   *Fig. 34*

METHOD: This routine is based on a coin vanish contributed by William Ball to a magic magazine called *The Sphinx*. Beforehand stick a small square of double-sided cellophane tape to your sleeve just forward of the elbow, at a point indicated by the arrow in Figure 33. When you try out the trick you will see where to place the tape. Double-sided tape has the adhesive on both sides. It is available in stationery and office-supply stores.

Ask the spectator to tear out a piece of a newspaper page. He should note the major headline on the paper so he will recognize it when you hand it back later. Crumple it up. Place it on your arm near the tape but not on the tape, as shown in Figure 33. Snap your hand downward and catch the paper, Figure 34. This stunt can be mastered with just a few minutes' practice. The trick is to drop your hand straight down.

Bring your hand up, Figure 35, keeping your right arm against your side. Your left side should be turned to the audience so that their view of the trick is the same as indicated in Figures 33, 34 and 35. Open your right hand to show that you've caught the paper.

Take the paper in your left hand and replace it on your right arm, just as in Figure 33, but this time place it directly onto the tape. Bear down so that the paper adheres firmly to the tape.

Snap your hand down and pretend to have caught the paper. Actually it will adhere to the back of the arm, thanks to the tape. Bring your right hand up, keeping your elbow against your side. Open your right hand to show that the paper has vanished.

Reach into your right trouser pocket as if to retrieve the paper. As you do, turn so that you face the audience directly. In the same motion, reach behind your back with your left hand and take the paper, Figure 36.

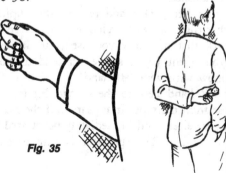

Fig. 35   *Fig. 36*

Your right hand comes out of your pocket without the paper. Act puzzled. Then reach into your left rear trouser pocket with your left hand and pretend to remove the paper from that pocket. Hand it back to the spectator so he can verify it's the same paper he gave you at the start.

The principle used in this routine lends itself to another approach when you are seated at the table, described as follows.

7 MATCHES TO GO

A spectator initials the inside of a matchbook. The magician places it on his elbow and tries to catch it. The matchbook vanishes. It is found in the magician's pocket.

He explains how it's done: He uses his sleeves. So saying, he drops the matchbook down his sleeve, whereupon it penetrates the sleeve. The spectator verifies the initials on the packet.

METHOD: Needed are two identical matchbooks. Have one in your left outside jacket pocket, the other in your right outside jacket pocket. There is a square of double-sided tape on your right elbow.

Remove the matchbook from your right pocket and have the spectator initial the inside of the flap. Close the matchbook and place it on your right sleeve near the elbow. Perform the catch stunt described in "Catching the News" (No. 6). Then place the matchbook on your sleeve, but directly onto the tape. Bear down so it adheres to the tape firmly.

Go through the motions of catching the matchbook, this time with your left side to the audience. Bring your right hand up to the position of Figure 35. Open your hand to show that the matchbook has vanished.

Reach into your left pocket and remove the duplicate matchbook, saying that the matches traveled over there. To explain how it's done, remark that of course you use your sleeves. Drop the packet down your right jacket sleeve. Pretend to work it down toward your elbow with your left hand.

When your left hand gets to the elbow, Figure 37, pull the matchbook loose from the tape. It appears as if the matchbook was dropped down your sleeve and immediately penetrated it. Toss the matches onto the table. The spectator is sure to check for his initials.

You can later drop your right hand to your side and allow the duplicate matchbook to fall secretly into your palm. Put the matches away when no one is looking.

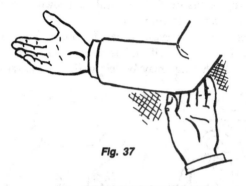

Fig. 37

8 PENDRAGON RINGS

Using two cardboard rings the magician demonstrates how spirit forces can be made to exert their influence when the spectator is not looking.

The cardboard rings are in a paper bag at the start of the trick. One of them is removed and slipped over the spectator's left arm. He is asked to clasp his hands tightly together, Figure 38. Now it is impossible to get the ring off the spectator's arm without tearing the ring.

The spectator is asked to close his eyes to allow the bashful spirits an interval of darkness to work their wonders. When the spectator opens his eyes, the ring has removed itself from his arm and is now over his head, Figure 39.

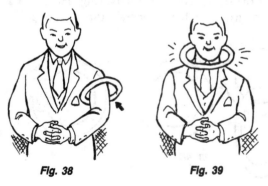

Fig. 38   *Fig. 39*

The second ring is removed from the bag and slipped over the spectator's left arm. The spectator places his left hand against his hip or hooks his left fingers around his belt. Then he places his right hand on top of his head. The result is shown in Figure 40. Each hand firmly traps one ring.

The spectator closes his eyes. When he opens them, the ring around his arm has freed itself and is now *linked* onto the other ring, Figure 41. Both rings may be left with the spectator at the finish.

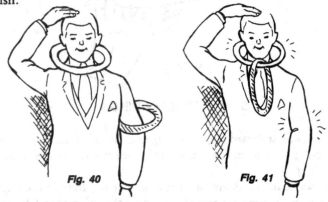

Fig. 40   Fig. 41

METHOD: The secret is partially a swindle in that you are always one step ahead of the spectator. A linked set of two cardboard rings is required. If the rings are cut from cardboard, it will be necessary to cut one ring, link it to the other ring, and then seal the cut ring with tape or staples.

Also required is a ring that is cut as shown in Figure 42. All three rings are in the paper bag at the start.

To present the trick, remove the loose ring. Hold it as shown in Figure 43, so that your hand conceals the slot. Slip it over the

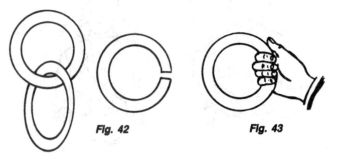

Fig. 42   Fig. 43

spectator's arm, Figure 44, so that the slot is in back and is concealed from the audience's view. Have the spectator clasp his hands together to make it impossible for you to get the ring off his arm.

When he closes his eyes, remove the cut ring by spreading open the gap and slipping the cut ring off his arm. Return it to the bag and remove the linked set of two.

Slip the linked set of two over his head but with the second ring hanging down in back, Figure 45. When the spectator opens his eyes he is greeted with the situation shown in Figure 39. The ring has left his arm and now appears around his neck.

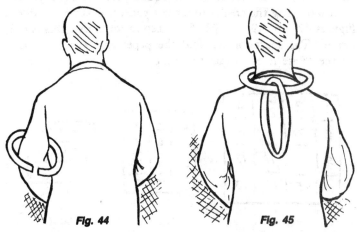

Fig. 44   Fig. 45

Remove the cut ring from the bag, holding it as shown in Figure 43 to conceal the slot. Slip it over his left arm with the slot in back. Have him hook the fingers of his left hand around his belt to trap the ring on his arm. Then have him put his right hand on his head to trap the other ring.

When the spectator closes his eyes, remove the cut ring from his arm, fold it and place it in your jacket pocket or somewhere else where it will be out of sight. Bring the linked ring from behind the spectator's back to the position shown in Figure 41.

The spectator opens his eyes. Not only has the ring freed itself from his left arm, but it has linked itself to the ring around his neck. All may be examined.

If other spectators are present, have them close their eyes at the appropriate times and they too will be fooled.

9 PARADOX PAPERS

This ingenious principle was introduced to magic by Martin Gardner. Get a piece of paper about the size of typewriter paper (8½" by 11") and fold it twice each way. When the paper is opened, it will contain 16 squares as shown in Figure 46. It is a good idea to fold the paper both ways along the creases for easy refolding later on.

Number the squares 1 to 16 as shown in Figure 46, that is, 1–2–3–4 from left to right, then 5–6–7–8 from right to left, and so on. When you have numbered the squares, fold up the paper any random way along the creases to make a packet. A sample is shown in Figures 47, 48, 49, 50, 51, 52. Keep in mind that this is only a sample. The spectator can fold the paper any way he chooses along the crease lines to make a packet.

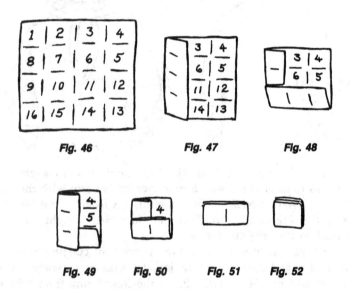

Fig. 46   Fig. 47   Fig. 48

Fig. 49   Fig. 50   Fig. 51   Fig. 52

Trim all four sides of the packet, Figure 53. Now deal the 16 pieces into a row on the table. You will observe a remarkable result. All the even-numbered pieces will be face up, all the odd-numbered pieces face down (or vice versa, depending on the way the paper is folded). This result is always obtained, no matter how the paper is folded.

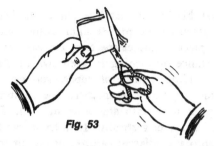

Fig. 53

There are many ways to exploit the principle. For example, give a spectator the ♦ A through ♦ 5 and have him choose one card. Say he takes the ♦ 4. Jot the names of the cards on one side of the paper, placing the names on the even-valued squares shown in Figure 54.

			◇A
	◇4		
		◇5	
◇2		◇3	

Fig. 54

The name of the chosen card (♦ 4) is placed on an odd-valued square. Since these are red cards, jot down their names with a red pencil.

Have another spectator choose a card from a packet consisting of the ♣ A through ♣ 5. Say he picks the ♣ 3. Turn over the paper side for side (left to right). Jot down the names of the clubs on the blank side of the paper. This time use a black pencil. Enter the names in the odd-valued squares, but enter the name of the chosen card (♣ 3) in an even-valued square.

Have the spectator fold the paper any way he chooses. Trim around the four sides of the folded packet or have him do it. Deal the pieces and you will discover a curious result. As the pieces are dealt, only red cards will show except for the chosen black card. Gather all the pieces and turn them over. Scatter them about on the table. Now only black cards will show except for the chosen red card. Because you have used different-color pencils, the result is visually striking.

A similar trick can be done with playing cards. Use eight reds and eight blacks. Deal them out face up in a four-by-four array so that reds and blacks alternate, as on a checkerboard. Have a spectator choose any red card. He signifies his choice by turning it face down in place. Another spectator chooses any black card. He signifies his choice by turning it face down in place.

Instead of folding a piece of paper, you gather the cards by flipping them over onto one another. The spectator starts at any card and flips it over onto any adjacent card. The card can be adjacent horizontally or vertically. Then these two cards are flipped over as one onto any adjacent card. Continue in this way until all 16 cards have been gathered.

Spread the packet out on the table. All of the red cards will be face up except for one face-up black card. This will be the chosen black card. Gather the cards, turn them over and spread the packet. Now all the face-up cards will be black except for one red card. This will be the chosen red card.

MONEY MAGIC

If you perform tricks with money you will always draw a crowd. Money is a commodity of universal interest. Most of the tricks in this chapter use paper money as the major apparatus. The tricks range from telepathy to teleportation. Some of the routines require prepared bills. In such cases it is best to use realistic play money of the kind found in novelty stores. The prepared bills can be carried in your wallet. Thus equipped, you are always ready to perform striking magic with paper money.

10 MIND vs. MONEY

This mind-reading routine uses no gimmicks or apparatus other than what the audience sees. The magician explains that he would like five people to stand and hold dollar bills aloft. The bills will be collected for a test of mind-reading skill. Rather than take up time later in returning the bills to their respective owners, the magician goes into the audience and gives each participant a dollar bill in exchange for the one collected.

The bills are collected. Each spectator gets a dollar bill in exchange for the bill he gives the magician. The packet of bills is handed directly to another spectator. There are no switches. Only one packet of bills is used.

The spectator mixes the bills. He gives one to the magician behind the magician's back. It can be any bill. Without asking a question or at any time glimpsing the bill handed to him, the magician immediately reveals the serial number on the bill.

The process is repeated with any bill handed to the magician behind his back. He may be genuinely blindfold by having a paper bag placed over his head. Despite the test conditions, the magician correctly reveals the serial number on every bill handed to him.

METHOD: The only requirement is a packet of six dollar bills. Jot down the serial numbers on a piece of paper. This done, the bills must be marked in some way so that they can be distinguished from one another by touch.

A simple method is to tear the first bill along one long edge by putting a ¼″ tear in it near the center of the long edge. Put a ¼″ tear in the center of a short edge of a second bill. Put two tears in the long edge of a third bill, and two tears in the short edge of a fourth bill. Don't tear the fifth bill.

Now any bill can be distinguished from any other even if the bills are turned over or handed to you upside down.

Other methods include pin-pricking each bill or bending down the corners. When devising a method of marking the bills, strive for a method that is simple and surefire. Once the bills are marked, the preparation is complete.

To perform, ask five spectators to stand. Approach the first spectator. Hand him an unprepared bill that you've previously placed on top of the stack. Take his bill in exchange. Place this bill on top of the stack.

Walk over to the second spectator. Take the top bill of the stack and give this to the second spectator. Take his bill in exchange and put it on top of the stack. Note that in giving the second spectator the top bill, you are giving him the bill you just got from the first spectator.

As you go from spectator to spectator, you are simply exchanging the top bill for each bill given to you by the previous spectator. Thus it is *only* the top bill of the packet that changes hands.

Once the last spectator has exchanged bills with you, take the top bill as if to hand it to someone else. Then remark that you have enough. The bill in hand is placed into your pocket. Hand the other five bills to any spectator for mixing. The bill you pocketed is the only unprepared bill in the stack. It is the one just received from the fifth spectator.

Turn your back. Your list of serial numbers is on a small piece of paper which is unobtrusively placed on the table, hidden behind some other object. When a dollar bill is handed to you behind your back, run your hands along the surface of the bill. This is perfectly acceptable to the audience because you are attempting to read the serial number by touch alone. As you examine the bill, run your fingertips along the edges. In this way you determine which bill has been handed to you. Consult the list to find out the serial number.

Repeat this with each of the other bills. When you get to the final bill it is not necessary to hold it in your hands. It will be the one with the serial number not yet called out. In this case have the spectator hold it and concentrate on the number. Then reveal it in an impressive manner.

If a paper bag is placed over your head, the task is even easier. Simply have the serial numbers written in pencil inside the paper bag. If you face into a light it is easy to see the serial numbers. It isn't too much trouble to memorize the numbers. Each serial number contains eight digits. Commit them to memory as if the digits formed two four-digit telephone numbers. Since you use the same bills over and over, once you have memorized the serial numbers, your work is done. This routine was devised by the author.

11 DOUBLE YOUR MONEY

This is a clever method of causing one dollar bill to look like two. Once the method has been learned, many uses will suggest themselves. It's best to use a crisp new dollar bill. Fold it in half lengthwise. Crease it sharply, then open it. Now crease the bill sharply across the middle and open it. This crease and those described below should be folded both ways to increase flexibility.

Using a knife or scissors, cut a slit in the center of the bill along the horizontal crease. The slit should run to the edges of the portrait of George Washington. The result will look like Figure 55. The slit is about 1¼″ in length.

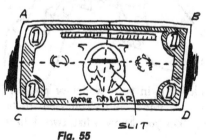

Fig. 55

Now fold or crease the bill from the right end of the slit to a point about an inch from the right of the top right corner of the bill. Open out the bill and form another crease from the left end of the slit to a point about an inch from the bottom left corner of the bill. Open out the bill. It will look like Figure 56.

Fold the bill in half the long way so that A–B is in back of C–D. Grasp the folded bill at the ends as shown in Figure 57.

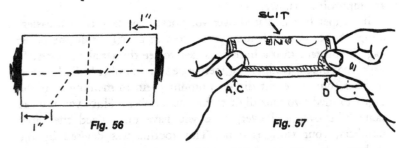

Fig. 56   Fig. 57

Move your right hand toward your left hand. The slit will open up as shown in Figure 58. Continue moving your right hand toward the left and downward. The bill will fold along the creases. The result is shown in Figure 59. It appears as if you have two bills, one lying on top of the other and at right angles to it.

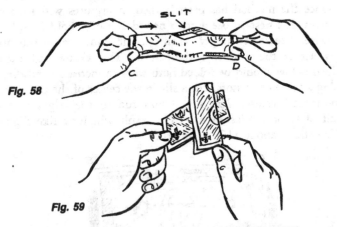

Fig. 58

Fig. 59

Keep the folded bill in your wallet or pocket. When ready to perform, remove the folded bill. You seem to have two bills in your hand. Say, "Do you know what two dollars will buy these days?"

Grasp the bill as in Figure 59 and move your hands apart. "About a dollar's worth of goods." As you say this, the bill straightens out. Two bills have magically become one. Unfold the bill and display it as shown in Figure 55. The slit will not be visible to the audience.

Another use for the bill is shown in the following psychic trick.

12 X MARKS THE SPOT

The magician places four dollars into a glass. Then he shows several slips of paper. Each is a diagram of a room in the house, Figure 60. The spectator chooses a room and marks a spot in that room with an X. Say he puts an X next to the chair in the living room. Instantly one of the dollar bills vanishes from the glass and teleports itself to the chair in the living room!

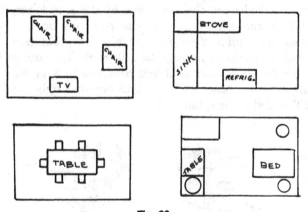

Fig. 60

METHOD: Required are floor plans of different rooms in your home, one room to each piece of paper. The plans do not have to be elaborate or detailed, just as long as they clearly show the placement of furniture. Four of them are as shown in Figure 60. The fifth has an X near, say, a chair, as shown in Figure 61. Place this sketch under a piece of cardboard and hold it in place with a large paper clip or bulldog clip, as shown in Figure 62.

Place the other floor plans on top of the cardboard, secured by the bulldog clip as shown in Figure 63. To complete this part of

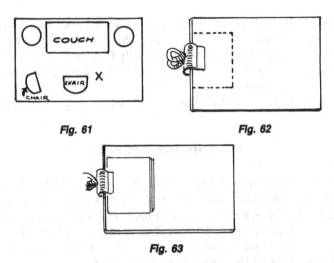

Fig. 61   *Fig. 62*

Fig. 63

the preparation, fold up a dollar bill and secretly place it in the living room under the chair indicated by the X in Figure 61.

A bill is constructed to look like two bills by the method described in "Double Your Money" (No. 11). Fold each of two other bills in quarters. Display the bills to the spectator as shown in Figure 64. It appears as if you have two bills in each hand. Actually your left hand holds two bills but your right hand holds one bill folded to look like two.

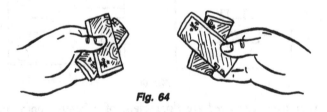

Fig. 64

Drop the bills from your left hand into a glass. Drop the bill from your right hand in on top. As you do this, say, "We'll put all four bills into this glass."

The four floor plans are fanned and shown to the audience. Then they are returned under the bulldog clip. Patter for a moment about teleportation.

Remove the bulldog clip from the cardboard. Take all five of the room floor plans, including the one concealed beneath the cardboard. Hand them to the spectator to place behind his back. Tell him to mix them well.

Then hand him a pen and tell him to place an X on the topmost floor plan behind his back. The pen is one that has run out of ink, so it doesn't matter where he makes the X. After he's done this, have him mix the floor plans again. Take the pen from him and put it in your pocket.

Then take the floor plans. Find the one with the X. In our example this would be the living room. Say, "You put an X near the easy chair opposite the couch."

Put the floor plans aside. Give the glass a shake. Remove the prepared bill and open it out, saying, "One." Remove another bill and open it out, saying "Two." Slowly remove the last bill and open it out, saying, "Three."

The fourth bill has vanished. Say, "I tried to teleport it to the room you chose." Let the spectator go to the living room. He will find the vanished dollar right at the spot indicated by the X.

13 DOLLAR FLIGHT

In this routine a one-dollar bill changes places with a five-dollar bill. When the trick is repeated there is a surprise ending.

Needed are a one-dollar bill, a five-dollar bill and two ordinary envelopes. The envelopes should be large enough to cover the bills easily. Seal the flaps of the envelopes so that the flaps don't get in the way of the handling.

Hold the dollar bill so Washington's picture is on the underside. The bill is folded in quarters by folding it first in half from right to left, and then folding it again from right to left. Make the creases sharp so the bill stays folded. Fold the five-dollar bill the same way. Place the dollar on the left, the five-dollar bill on the right. Grasp one envelope in your left hand between thumb and forefinger. Grasp the other envelope in your right hand between forefinger and middle finger. Figure 65 shows the starting position.

Cover each bill with an envelope. Without letting go of the envelopes, pick up the bills under the envelopes. Hold the dollar bill against its envelope with the aid of your left forefinger. Hold

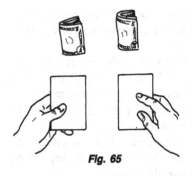

Fig. 65

the five-dollar bill under its envelope with the aid of your right middle finger. The situation is shown in Figure 66.

Bring your hands together so that the left-hand envelope is above the right-hand envelope. The top envelope and the dollar bill are now grasped between your right thumb and forefinger. Simultaneously the bottom envelope and the five-dollar bill are clipped between your left forefinger and middle finger, Figure 67.

Separate your hands, Figure 68. Then immediately cross them, Figure 69, and leave the apparatus on the table. The above changeover, devised by Sam Horowitz and Jacob Daley, makes it seem that the five-dollar bill has been placed on the left. Ask the spectator, "Under which envelope is the five-dollar bill?"

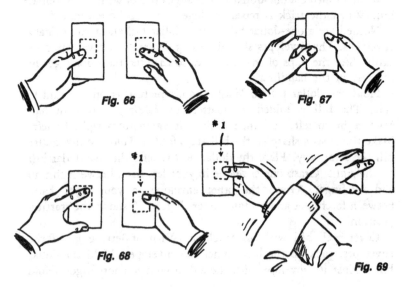

Fig. 66

Fig. 67

Fig. 68

Fig. 69

He will almost always point to the left-hand envelope. Lift the left-hand envelope to show the dollar bill on the left. Then lift the right-hand envelope to show the five-dollar bill on the right. This completes the first phase of the routine; the bills have unexpectedly changed places.

Offer to show just how it works. You are now back at the position of Figure 65. Grasp the envelopes as in Figure 65, then pick up the bills under the envelopes as in Figure 66. Bring your hands together exactly as shown in Figure 67, the left-hand envelope being above the right-hand envelope.

The change in handling occurs at this point. As your hands are separated, your left hand takes only the bottom envelope. This means that both bills will be under the right-hand envelope. The dollar bill will be held against the right-hand envelope by your right forefinger. The five-dollar bill will be clipped under the right-hand envelope between the right forefinger and middle finger.

Cross your hands as in Figure 69. Release the left-hand envelope. Then release the five-dollar bill and let it fall to the table at the left, Figure 70. Remark that you really palmed the five all along.

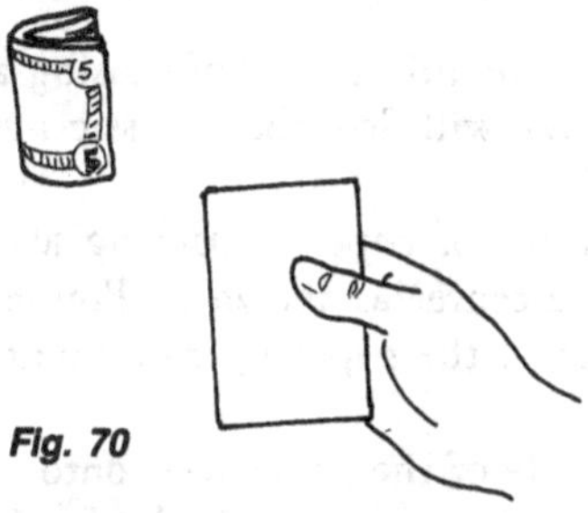

Fig. 70

Your right hand replaces its envelope on top of the five-dollar bill. The trick is apparently over. Then say, almost as an afterthought, "By the way, do you know where the dollar bill is?" The spectator will point to the right-hand envelope. Lift it to show no bill. Then lift the other envelope to show that both bills are under that envelope.

An even stronger finish can be achieved with a bit more preparation. In this case, at the finish the dollar bill appears *inside* one of the sealed envelopes. At the start seal a duplicate dollar bill inside the right-hand envelope. Then proceed with the routine up to the point of Figure 70. Your left hand now grasps the right-hand envelope, thumb on top, fingers below, Figure 71, and places this envelope into the jacket pocket. The dollar bill is concealed behind the envelope.

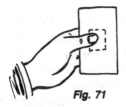

Fig. 71

You have just gotten to the point in the trick where you remark that you palmed the five-dollar bill. Then say, "By the way, where's the dollar bill?" The spectator may point to the envelope on the table. Lift it up, turn it over, act surprised that the dollar bill has vanished. Then tear open the envelope and slowly remove the dollar bill from inside.

14 THE COIN FOLD

The coin fold is a useful method of causing a coin or other small object to vanish. We will describe a classic method that has many uses.

Begin with a piece of paper measuring about 5″ square. Place the coin just above center as shown in Figure 72.

Fold the bottom of the paper up to a point about ½″ from the top, Figure 73.

Fold the right side of the paper over onto the back, Figure 74. Then fold the left side over onto the back, Figure 75.

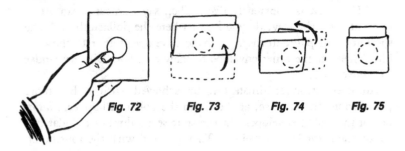

Fig. 72   *Fig. 73*   *Fig. 74*   *Fig. 75*

Finally, fold the top ½″ down in back as shown in Figure 76. The coin appears to be securely wrapped inside the paper. Unknown to the audience there is an opening at the top through which the coin can escape.

The usual method of stealing the coin is to turn the folded paper around so that the opening is at the bottom. Hold the folded paper in your right hand as in Figure 77. Release pressure and the coin will slide out into your hand.

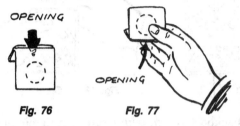

Fig. 76   Fig. 77

Grasp the folded paper with your left hand. Your right hand, with the palmed coin, goes into your pocket, leaves the coin behind, then comes out of the pocket with invisible wuffle dust. Sprinkle the dust over the paper, then tear the paper to show that the coin has vanished.

A dollar bill can be used in place of the paper. First fold the bill in half so that it is more nearly square in shape. Then proceed with the coin fold exactly as described above.

A method where the coin does not have to be palmed is described in the next trick.

15 BANK BY MAIL

The bank of the future will use instant methods of depositing money. The magician demonstrates one such method. A coin is wrapped inside a bank deposit slip. It vanishes immediately and is found inside the magician's bankbook.

METHOD: Place two quarters inside a bankbook, one above the other. Hold them in place by clipping a pen to the bankbook as shown in Figure 78. This is the only advance preparation. Blank deposit slips can be obtained from any bank. They make the trick look more authentic but are not absolutely necessary; any official-looking piece of paper can be used since it will be torn up anyway.

Have the bankbook in your pocket until you are ready to perform. Then remove it and grasp it with your right hand. Your right thumb presses against the upper coin, holding it in place.

Your left hand removes the pen, allowing the bottom coin to fall to the table as shown in Figure 79.

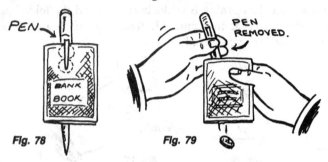

Fig. 78   **Fig. 79**

Place the bankbook down, taking care to maintain pressure until the book is on the table. This way the concealed coin won't fall out. The audience should be unaware that there is a quarter inside the bankbook.

Remark that in the future banks will use teleportation to aid in depositing money. As you speak, take a deposit slip from your pocket. Wrap the visible quarter in it, but use the coin fold described in the previous trick. The folded slip with the quarter inside is placed into your outer jacket pocket, Figure 80, with the open side of the paper downward. The result is that the coin will silently slip out of the paper into your pocket.

Fig. 80

"All I have to do is say the magic words 'Compound Interest,' " you remark. As you say this, wave the pen over your pocket and over the bankbook. Remove the paper from your pocket and tear it to bits to show that the coin has vanished. Then tip the bankbook, allowing the coin to slide out into view. The coin has magically traveled from the deposit slip to the bankbook.

16 SLOW-MOTION MONEY

A one-dollar bill put under the spectator's hand changes places with a five-dollar bill held by the magician. This clever trick was marketed by U. F. Grant. It gets its name from the fact that all moves are performed slowly. The handling is completely fair, yet the bills change places instantly.

METHOD: Because money is to be cut and pasted, use play money for this trick. In the upper-right corner of a five-dollar bill is the number 5 with a circle around it. Cut out this circle, Figure 81, and paste it onto the upper-right corner of a one-dollar bill, Figure 82. This is the only preparation. Keep this bill tucked away in a compartment of your wallet so you don't accidentally spend it.

To present the trick, remove the prepared bill from your wallet along with an ordinary five-dollar bill. Hold the prepared bill as shown in Figure 83, with your thumb over the prepared corner, so that the bill can be shown on both sides.

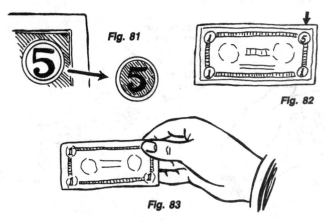

Fig. 81

Fig. 82

Fig. 83

Hold up the one-dollar bill with the prepared side toward you. Slowly fold it in half, Figure 84, by bringing the left side around in back of the right side. Then fold the bill once more in half by bringing the left side around in back of the right side, Figure 85. Finally, fold the bill in half by bringing the bottom edge up in back of the top, Figure 86. At all times the prepared corner faces you. The spectators see only that you have folded a one-dollar bill in eighths. Place this bill on the table with the prepared corner underneath.

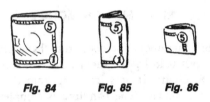

Fig. 84   **Fig. 85**   **Fig. 86**

Now pick up the five-dollar bill and freely show it on both sides. Fold it in eighths exactly as you did the dollar bill.

Place both bills on your right palm, Figure 87. Tell the spectator to place his right hand palm down on the table. Hold both bills in place with your thumb. Then turn your hand palm down. This has the effect of turning both bills over in your hand. Now the prepared corner of the one-dollar bill is uppermost.

With the aid of your thumb, push the five-dollar bill under the spectator's hand. Don't let him see which bill he gets. Then display the other bill with the prepared corner uppermost, Figure 88. It appears as if you hold the five-dollar bill.

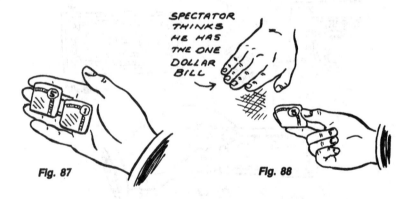

SPECTATOR THINKS HE HAS THE ONE DOLLAR BILL

Fig. 87   **Fig. 88**

Place this bill in your pocket. Snap your fingers. Have the spectator open his hand. Now he holds the five-dollar bill. It is a startling trick.

To finish, you have only to bring out the prepared bill and unfold it. Display it as in Figure 83. If you wish, you can have an unprepared dollar bill folded in eighths in your pocket beforehand. At the end of the trick leave the prepared bill in your pocket and bring out the unprepared dollar bill. With this approach both bills are unprepared and may be examined by the audience.

17 THE DOLLAR-BILL RING

This is the classic method of making a finger ring out of a dollar bill. It ends up with the number 1 as the signet. Following a description of the way the ring is made, a trick using the dollar-bill ring will be given.

Use a crisp new dollar bill. Make sure the creases are sharp. Begin by holding the bill with Washington's picture uppermost. Fold in the upper and lower white borders, Figure 89.

Fold the top half down, Figure 90. Then fold the bill in half again, Figure 91. Turn the bill lengthwise and fold down the white border of the bill as in Figure 92. Then fold down the top ¾", Figure 93. This is the portion with the word "one." The "one" will later be the setting in the ring.

Turn the bill over, Figure 94, and fold the bottom 2" up in the direction of the arrow. The result is shown in Figure 95. We will refer to this 2" section as flap X.

Fold flap X along the dotted diagonal line in Figure 95 to the position shown in Figure 96.

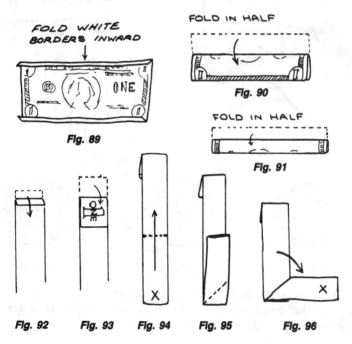

Fig. 89

FOLD WHITE BORDERS INWARD

ONE

FOLD IN HALF

Fig. 90

FOLD IN HALF

Fig. 91

Fig. 92   Fig. 93   Fig. 94   Fig. 95   Fig. 96

Turn the bill around and place it against your left forefinger, Figure 97. The top section of the bill is brought around behind your forefinger and up in front, in the direction of the arrows. The result to this point is shown in Figure 98.

With the bill in the position of Figure 98, release the portion with the "one" so that it flips up, Figure 99. Now bring flap X over to the right in the direction of the arrow in Figure 99. The result is shown in Figure 100.

Bring the portion with the setting down in the direction of the arrow in Figure 100. The white margin is then tucked in as shown in Figure 101. Flap X is then brought inside the ring and tucked into the diagonal pocket shown in Figure 102. The result is the ring shown in Figure 103.

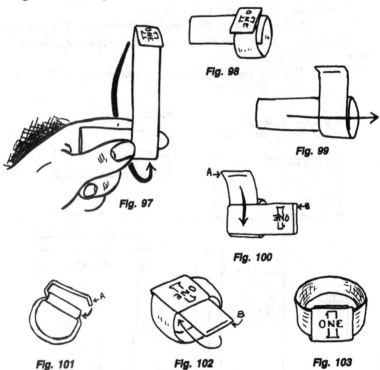

Fig. 98

Fig. 99

Fig. 97

Fig. 100

Fig. 101

Fig. 102

Fig. 103

If you want to impress friends with your ability to make a ring out of a dollar bill, prefold the bill as described above, then open it out and carry it with you. The ring can later be constructed rapidly from the prefolded bill. A quick trick using the dollar-bill ring is described next.

18 REAL OR COUNTERFEIT?

One spectator places the dollar-bill ring in his hand and closes his hand into a fist. A second spectator removes his own ring, and clenches it in his closed fist. All of this is done while the magician has his back turned.

Either spectator steps behind the magician. The magician touches the spectator's clenched fist and immediately announces whether this party has the real ring or the dollar-bill ring.

METHOD: Spot someone who wears a signet ring on his right hand. Ask him to assist. Then pick a spectator who wears a plain ring on his right hand and have him assist. Drop the dollar-bill ring on the table and turn your back.

Remark that you can tell real jewelry from counterfeit by a highly developed sense of touch. Ask either spectator to remove his ring silently and hold it in his clenched right hand. Then have the other spectator hide the dollar-bill ring in his clenched right hand. Each spectator now has a ring.

Either party steps behind you and extends his closed right hand. Reach behind your back and touch the spectator's hand. Pretend you are getting psychic vibrations. As you slide your hand over the spectator's, determine by touch if he is wearing his own ring. If so, he must have the dollar-bill ring in his clenched fist.

Now you know what the spectator is holding but you don't know which spectator he is. Recall that at the beginning you chose someone who wore a signet ring and someone else who wore a plain ring. As soon as you touch the ring you know if it has a signet. This tells you the spectator's identity and allows you to reveal the information in a dramatic way. One example is as follows: "This is a well-dressed fellow who smokes a pipe and drives a late-model car. He holds in his hand a ring worth considerably more than a dollar."

If the spectator is not wearing a ring, it means he has his ring clenched in his fist. Have the other spectator then step behind you. Find out by the above method which spectator he is, then go on with the revelation.

PSYCHIC MYSTERIES

Psychic and mind-reading tricks are among the most compelling in the literature. Unlike many conjuring routines in which the audience assumes there's a trick involved, people tend to believe in the reality of telepathy.

This chapter contains a number of mind-reading tricks using paper. The apparatus ranges from paper bags to paperback books. A complete act could be built around these tricks. It would be lightweight and portable, yet the act would be impressive to laymen.

19 PSYCHOMETRIC DETECTIVE

If you have been asked to perform a trick and have no apparatus with you, this excellent routine of Jules Lenier's is just the ticket. In this routine four people become characters in a murder mystery. With the aid of psychometry you solve the crime and determine the part taken by each spectator.

METHOD: The secret is simple and depends on a classic method of secretly marking several pieces of paper. All the work is done by the spectators. Take a large rectangular sheet of paper and have a spectator tear it in half. The spectator takes one of the torn pieces and tears it in half. Then he takes one of these torn pieces and tears it in quarters. The result is shown in Figure 104.

Without knowing it, the spectator has marked each of the small pieces so each can later be identified at a glance. The system is this:

No. 1 has four rough edges.
No. 2 has one long smooth edge.
No. 3 has one short smooth edge.
No. 4 has two smooth edges.

Hand out the small slips to four different spectators. Make sure you hand out the pieces of paper in order so you will later know who got which piece. On the large piece of paper marked A in Figure 104, draw the legend shown in Figure 105.

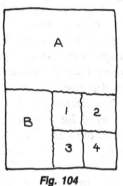

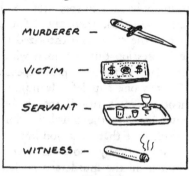

| **Fig. 104** | **Fig. 105** |

While your back is turned, have one spectator silently volunteer to be the servant, another the victim, another the witness and another the murderer. The murderer draws a picture of the murder weapon, a knife in Figure 105, on his piece of paper. The victim draws a picture of the stolen loot—a dollar bill—on his piece of paper. The witness draws a picture of the cigarette found at the scene of the crime on his piece of paper. The servant draws a picture of a serving tray on his piece of paper.

After this has been done, the victim gives his piece of paper to the murderer, who in turn puts it into his pocket. The other slips are mixed and placed on the table.

You have no idea which spectator chose which role. While your back is turned take the paper marked B and tear it in half. On one piece write the word "Subpoena." On the other write your name and phone number, as if the paper were a business card.

Glancing at the slips, pick up the servant's slip. It might be the slip with one short smooth edge. This is slip no. 3 in Figure 104. Since the slips were passed out in order originally, you know who got slip no. 3. This in turn means that you know who volunteered to play the role of the servant. Give a short reading, saying something like, "The servant was on duty the night his boss bumped off the victim. I get the impression he's tall, wears glasses and favors brown shoes." You have simply described spectator no. 3. Turn to him and say, "You are the servant." Hand him the slip of paper with your phone number, explaining that, since he will need a new job, he can use your name as a reference.

Now pick up the witness' slip. This may be the slip with four rough edges. You therefore know that this slip was the one originally handed to spectator no. 1. Pretend to mull over psycho-metric thoughts, then say, "The police found a cigarette at the scene of the crime and theorized it belonged to the witness. I get the impression this is a man who enjoys sports and wears a blue suit." Turn to the appropriate spectator and hand him the subpoena.

There's one slip left. It might be the slip that has one long smooth edge, a tip-off that it belongs to spectator no. 2. You know that he's the murderer, but don't reveal his identity yet. Instead, note that since you know the owners of three of the slips, you automatically know the victim's identity even though his slip is hidden in the murderer's pocket.

Say, "The victim is of course the silent man in all of this. But if he could speak he would tell you that he lost his life over a few dollars stolen from the pocket of his gray tweed jacket." Here you describe the clothes worn by the victim. Then conclude by saying, "He knows what many suspected." Point dramatically to the murderer and say, "That *he* is the guilty man!"

20 THE HOMETOWN TEST

Everyone has feelings of nostalgia for the town in which they grew up. This trick incorporates the hometown theme into a feat of mind reading.

The magician distributes blank envelopes to a dozen different people in the audience. He asks each to address the envelope to a friend or relative in his hometown. The envelopes are then gathered and mixed in a paper bag.

The magician reaches into the bag and chooses an envelope at random. Turning his head away, he removes the envelope and holds it aloft. Slowly he reveals who this letter was addressed to. Then he reveals the name of the town. Finally, even though the envelope bears no return address, he correctly returns the envelope to the spectator who filled it out.

The trick is repeated with several more envelopes.

METHOD: The secret is based on a clever idea suggested by

Robert Parrish. Cut a window near the bottom of a paper bag as shown in Figure 106. Prepare another bag the same way and insert this bag into the first bag. This creates a double thickness so that an accidental backlight will not betray the presence of the window.

Fold the bottom of the bag up, Figure 107, and then fold the top down, Figure 108. The window is on the inside and is therefore concealed from view.

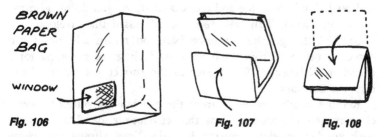

BROWN PAPER BAG

WINDOW

Fig. 106   **Fig. 107**   **Fig. 108**

You will also need a dozen envelopes and pencils to distribute to the audience. Each envelope is secretly marked. Put one nail nick on the top edge of the first envelope, two on the second and so on.

When distributing the envelopes, make sure the first spectator gets the envelope marked no. 1, the second spectator gets the envelope marked no. 2, etc. Have the spectators fill in the name and address of someone they might want to contact in their hometown. While the spectators do this, open the paper bag. Tell the spectators to turn the envelopes writing-side down. The envelopes are then collected in the bag. Keep the window concealed from audience view.

Place the bag on a table. Reach in with your right hand and mix the envelopes. Then grasp any envelope and hold it as in Figure 109 so that you can see the writing.

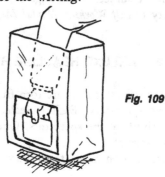

Fig. 109

As soon as you glimpse the name and address, turn your head aside to make it clear you are not looking at the envelope. Remove it from the bag and hold it aloft. Pretend to get mental impressions. Then reveal the information you glimpsed, but in an indirect way. For example, if the envelope is addressed to someone in Nebraska, mention that you get an impression of snow and ice, of long winters, sleigh rides and so on. Then look at the envelope and read aloud the name and address on it. As you do so, glimpse the secret marks. This tells you who addressed the envelope.

Say, "Although this envelope bears no return address, I can detect someone in this room who has feelings of nostalgia for a friend in Nebraska." Walk over to the correct person and hand him the envelope.

Remove another envelope from the bag but say you don't get a clear mental impression. Toss that envelope aside. Do the same with another envelope, tossing it aside. Then glimpse the name and address on the next envelope and go through a revelation similar to that given above.

Discard more envelopes until just one is left in the bag. Then give a final reading for that envelope.

If you lived near the town written on an envelope, you can interject direct and accurate descriptions of local landmarks. This adds to the mood you are trying to project, that of receiving mental flashes of distant places. When people think back to their hometown days, they invariably remember happy scenes from childhood memories of holidays and summer vacations. Use the trick of describing scenes from your own childhood when giving the supposed readings. Keep it general and upbeat. You will get credit for terrific mind-reading abilities.

For more on the subject of readings of this type, see the chapter on Psychometry in *Self-Working Mental Magic* (Dover 23806–7).

21 DELUXE HEADLINE READING

Several random news articles are torn from a borrowed newspaper by different spectators. Each is sealed in an envelope. The envelopes are mixed by the spectators. One envelope is chosen at random by any spectator.

The magician concentrates, then draws something on a large

sheet of paper. The envelope is opened by the spectator. The news article is read aloud. It is a story about an accident in which a car skidded out of control and hit a tree. The magician turns around the picture he drew. It shows a car hitting a tree.

METHOD: This trick can be done either close up or on a stage. Preparation is simple and can be accomplished in a few minutes.

From today's paper tear out four stories of a kind which can be told in pictures. Stories of fires, car chases and bank robberies are the kind of thing you should look for. Choose short articles. Tear them out so the tearing looks casual, but make sure you leave in the headline. You want brief stories so they won't take much space when folded. You want to include the headline so the audience can tell at a glance what the story is about.

Fold each story small enough so it just fits into an envelope. Then place each in a separate envelope. Remember which envelope contains which story. An easy way to do this is to arrange the stories alphabetically by subject. An example would be car chase, fire, murder, robbery. Then mark the envelopes by nicking them with your nail, so you can tell them apart.

Stack the envelopes one behind the other in order. Take an empty envelope and cut off the flap, Figure 110. Then place this envelope in front of the stack. Place three or four empty envelopes behind the ones that contain the stories. Finally place a rubber band around the package. Figure 111 shows how the apparatus looks.

REMOVE FLAP

Fig. 110

PACKAGE OF ENVELOPES

FLAPLESS
ENVELOPE
IN FRONT   **Fig. 111**

To present the trick, hand out pages from the newspaper to four different spectators. Ask each to tear his page in half, then in half again, then in half again. Each is to choose a torn piece and fold it into quarters.

When this has been done, take the first story and place it inside the top envelope of the stack. This is the flapless envelope. Ask the spectator for his initials. Openly write them on what seems to be the flap—the spectator is unaware that this is really the flap of the envelope directly in back of the prepared envelope.

Remove the initialed envelope from the stack, Figure 112, and hand it to the spectator. Tell him to seal the envelope and put his initials on the outside. He sees his initials on the flap of this envelope, so all appears fair. He is unaware that the story he gave the magician has been switched for another.

Fig. 112

Move on to the second spectator. Take the folded newspaper from him and put it inside the top envelope. This is the flapless envelope, which now contains two stories, one from each of the first two spectators. Jot down the second spectator's initials on the flap. Then remove the initialed envelope. This is the envelope just behind the prepared (flapless) envelope. Have the spectator seal the envelope and write his initials on the outside.

Proceed in exactly the same way with the third and fourth spectators. In each case their folded piece of paper goes into the flapless envelope. Each spectator thinks he is getting back his own newspaper clipping in an envelope he himself has signed and sealed. Actually each spectator gets one of the planted stories.

Have someone gather the envelopes and mix them. He chooses any envelope and holds it in plain view. From the nail nicks you know, for example, that this envelope belongs to the second spectator. Since he got the second planted story, you know this story was about a fire in a rooming house. On a large sheet of paper sketch a picture of a house with flames shooting out of the window. The picture need not be artistic.

Don't show your picture yet. Have the envelope opened. Let the spectator read the headline of the story. Then turn your picture around to show a correct match.

Pretend you can't get the next picture and the next. Draw something in each case but make sure it is at best only a vague match with the story inside the envelope. Then have the spectator hold up the final envelope. Sketch a picture of this story on a fresh sheet of paper. Have the envelope opened and the clipping read aloud. Turn your drawing around so it faces the audience. It is a correct match and a dramatic finish to the trick.

22 A NAME IN MILLIONS

A telephone directory is opened to a page. The spectator places one hand on top of the other, Figure 113, and closes his eyes. With his hands in the position of Figure 113 he places both hands on the page.

He separates his fingers slightly, Figure 114, and opens his eyes long enough to peer through his open fingers at the name he can see most clearly. Then he closes his eyes and concentrates on the name.

Fig. 113

Fig. 114

The magician stands some distance away. He concentrates for a moment, then says, "I think I have a mental picture of the party you chose. The family lives in a white frame house north of here. The father drives a Ford. I know the son, Tom Wilson. Is that the name you chose?"

The magician is correct.

METHOD: This is an audacious test which requires only a telephone directory and a lot of nerve. Unknown to the spectator, you open the directory to a page which is filled with the same name. Don't choose an obvious popular name like Smith or Jones. Flip through the directory to find a page which is filled with a less popular name like Wilson or Thompson.

Tell the spectator to close his eyes as you put the telephone directory on the table in front of him. Open it to the page that contains the same name repeated over and over. Have the spectator hold his hands as in Figure 113. Tell him to place his hands on the page. Then have him open his fingers just enough to allow him to see one name, Figure 114. He opens his eyes, glances at the name he sees and closes his eyes.

Have him close the directory. Explain that he must keep his eyes closed to aid in concentration. Give the above patter story. Note that you refer to the son, Tom Wilson. This is protect you from the chance that the spectator might note both the first and last names of the chosen party. By revealing the son's name, it doesn't matter that the spectator saw a different first name. When you ask if Wilson was the name the spectator chose, he must agree that it was the correct *last* name.

23 CELEBRITY SWEEPSTAKES

Ask the spectator to call out the names of celebrities on television. Jot down the names on different slips of paper. When you have a dozen or so slips, fold them and place them in a paper bag. Have a spectator shake the bag to mix the contents. On a blank piece of paper you write a prediction, change your mind and write another prediction.

The spectator reaches into the bag and removes any piece of paper. Your prediction is read and it correctly predicts the chosen television personality.

METHOD: This is a classic method of forcing a name. When performing the trick, borrow a pad and pencil. Ask for the names of different television celebrities. Say the first name called out is Hoffman and the second is Kellar.

Pretend to jot down the names of the television personalities as they are called out. Actually you write Hoffman on the first slip,

Kellar on the second, Hoffman on the third, Kellar on the fourth, and so on.

Fold the slips and drop them into a paper bag. On the pad write Hoffman as your prediction, then cross it out by putting a single line through it. Under it write Kellar.

Have someone remove any piece of paper from the bag. They open the slip and read the chosen name aloud. If it matches the second name you wrote, take a bow. If it matches the crossed-out name, explain that you had it but changed your mind. It's still an impressive feat.

24 LOCKED THOUGHTS

This trick uses a confederate but the secret is well concealed. A combination lock is given to the spectators to examine. They are told that the first two numbers in the combination are, for example, 32 left, 18 right. They are to guess the third number.

Each of the three spectators whispers his guess to the magician, who jots down the guesses on a pad. Each person knows his own number but not the others. When the three numbers have been jotted down, each person verifies that the number written is the number he actually chose.

The magician looks over the guesses and says that none of them is correct. But when a fourth spectator adds the numbers, the total is indeed the number required to open the combination lock.

METHOD: At no time does any spectator know the number chosen by any other spectator. This point alone should discourage the idea of a confederate since the confederate's number obviously has no bearing on the outcome.

The confederate is the first spectator. When he whispers a number to you, jot down his initials on the pad. Go to the second spectator. Make sure he can't see what you've written. Have him whisper a number to you. Jot it down on the pad. Do the same with the third spectator. Draw a line under the numbers. To this point the situation is as shown in Figure 115.

You know that the number 25, for example, is the correct third number required to open the combination lock. Mentally total the two numbers on the pad and subtract them from 25. The result in this example is 10.

Go back to the first spectator. Ask for his initials. Pretend to write them on the pad. Actually you write the number 10 next to his initials, Figure 116. The audience sees you write something. They assume it is the spectator's initials.

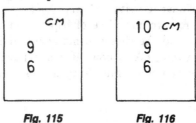

Fig. 115   Fig. 116

Go to the second spectator and ask for his initials. Write them next to his number. Write the third spectator's initials next to his number.

Hand the pad and pencil to a fourth spectator as you remark that the numbers you were given seem a bit too low. Ask the fourth party to total the numbers. When he's done this, have each of the other spectators verify that the addition is correct. In the process they also see that you wrote exactly the numbers they gave you.

To total is 25. Have a spectator turn the combination lock left to 25. Amazingly, the lock snaps open.

When asking for numbers, say that they should be low numbers. This way the total of the numbers in Figure 115 won't exceed 25. When all three numbers have been written on the pad, look at them and say "These numbers are a bit *too* low. Let's add them."

25 LITTLE ALBERT

Any book, magazine or newspaper supplied by the spectator can be used for this test. The magician supplies a paper bag and two blank cards.

On one of the cards the magician jots down a word he thinks the spectator will choose. He initials the back of this card and places it into the bag. The spectator then opens the book to any page and notes any word. Say the word is "chair." The magician jots down this word on the other blank card and writes the spectator's name on the back. This card is also dropped into the paper bag.

The magician reviews the conditions. The spectator could have chosen any book, opened it to any page and chosen any word. Then the magician turns over the paper bag. Both of the cards drop out onto the table. One card has the spectator's name on one side and the word "chair" on the other. The second card has the magician's name on one side and the word "chair" on the other, a perfect match.

You can make a spectacular mystery out of it by going with a friend to a public library. Tell him he can wander anywhere in the library, choose any book from any shelf and mentally select any word in the book. Though you could not possibly know which book he has selected, you still get the chosen word with complete accuracy.

METHOD: There is some slight preparation but it has nothing to do with the book. You need to know the name of the spectator who will participate. Say his name is John. Write his name on a blank card. Write your own name on the face of another blank card.

To complete the preparation, obtain a roll of double-sided (double-adhesive) transparent tape from a stationery store. This tape has a sticky surface on both sides. Cut off a square of tape and place it on the inside bottom of an ordinary paper bag. This completes the preparation.

Prior to presenting the trick arrange to have the paper bag mouth up on the table. Place the card with the spectator's name on your palm, writing-side up. On top of this place the card bearing your own name, writing-side down. On top of all place a blank card.

To perform the routine have the spectator take a book to a far corner of the room, open it to any page and select a word. Emphasize the freedom of choice.

While he concentrates, pretend to mull over thought waves you are receiving. Jot down a word on the upper surface of the top card on the stack. Turn over the card and write your name on the back. Place the card into the paper bag. Press down on it so it adheres to the double-sided tape inside the bag.

Now ask for the selected word. Jot it down on the top face of the cards in your hand. Turn both cards over as a unit and pretend to write the spectator's name on the blank side. Actually you write the chosen word again.

Keep the two cards together as you drop them into the paper bag. Review the fair conditions in selecting a word. Then tip the bag over and allow the two cards to fall out. Thanks to the tape, the extra card remains inside the bag, Figure 117.

CARD REMAINS IN BAG

Fig. 117

One card has the spectator's name on one side and the chosen word on the other. The second card has your name on one side and the same chosen word on the other.

There is a way to do the trick without tape inside the bag. This method also provides a logical reason for the use of a small paper bag. The bag is used to hold a supply of blank cards. Two of the cards are prepared as described above. These two cards are on top of the stack with a blank card on top of them.

When ready to perform the trick, remove these three cards. Place them in your hand as described above. The other blank cards are kept inside the bag. When the spectator goes to a far corner of the room and chooses a word from the book, pretend to write your thoughts on the upper surface of the top card. In fact you write nothing. Turn over the card and pretend to sign your name to it. Again write nothing. Drop this card into the paper bag.

Then complete the test as described above, writing the chosen word on both blank surfaces of the cards in hand. Drop them as a unit into the bag. At the finish tip over the bag and allow all the cards to fall out. There will be writing on two cards. All other cards will be blank. It will be seen that your word matches the spectator's.

This trick was devised by the author. The title was taken from the name of one of the infamous Black Books.

PAPER CAPERS

If you perform tricks often for friends, it is wise to have on hand a series of stunts and puzzles that can be used as a change of pace from magical routines. The stunts in this chapter are offbeat and different. Most have a connection to magic tricks. They are all constructed from paper or cardboard, so they are lightweight and easy to handle.

26 VISUALIZATION TEST

If you fold a square of paper, give it a single cut and open it out, how many holes would you expect to find in the paper? This elegant test of the spectator's powers of observation was devised by J. C. Coy. It produces a surprising result.

METHOD: Fold the paper in half four times as shown in Figures 118–122. Do this slowly so the spectator can observe each fold. Then cut off the upper right corner, shown as X–X in Figure 123. Ask the spectator how many holes the paper will have when it is unfolded.

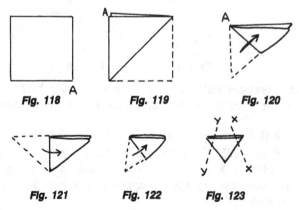

Fig. 118   Fig. 119   Fig. 120

Fig. 121   Fig. 122   Fig. 123

Most people think the answer is four. But when you unfold the paper, it will contain only one hole!

Offer to try another test. Slowly refold the paper along the original creases. Now cut the left corner, shown as Y–Y in Figure 123. Ask how many additional holes will be in the paper.

Surprisingly enough, the answer is none!

This stunt can be made the basis for a puzzling magical effect, as described next.

27 DECEPTA DIE

The magician folds up a plain square of paper and trims the corners. The spectator rolls a die on the table. Say he rolls the number 5.

The magician unfolds the paper to show that it contains five holes, exactly matching the number rolled by the spectator. The unfolded paper is shown in Figure 124.

METHOD: Fold up the paper exactly as described in "Visualization Test" (No. 26). As you do, hand the spectator an ordinary die and have him roll it several times to prove it isn't loaded. Then tell him to roll it one more time to pick a number.

At just this point you should have completed folding the paper. It is now in the shape shown in Figure 123. Cut through the corner Y–Y as shown in Figure 125. As you do, glance at the die to see which number was rolled.

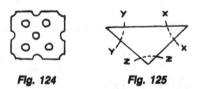

Fig. 124   Fig. 125

If the spectator rolled a 1, cut through corner X–X and open out the paper to show the paper contains the same number of holes.

If he rolled a 4, *don't* cut through X–X. Instead cut through Z–Z in Figure 125. Open the paper to show four holes.

If he rolled a 5, cut through X–X and then through Z–Z. When you open the paper it will appear as in Figure 124, with five holes showing.

If the spectator rolls any other number, tell him you will use the number on the underside of the die. Tell him to turn over the die. This will bring into view either the 1, the 4 or the 5.

For the trick to succeed it must appear that you follow a set cutting procedure regardless of the number thrown on the die. Time the handling so that you cut through Y–Y just as the spectator rolls the die the final time to choose a number. Glance at the number thrown without making it obvious. Then make the required cuts described above.

28 LIVING DOLL

The next time you know you are going to be served a cup of hot tea, cut out one or two small dolls from a piece of paper, Figure 126. Remark that tea has long been thought to contain magical properties, which is why tea leaves are used to give readings.

You show another magical property of tea with this curious feat. Cover the cup of tea with a handkerchief or cloth napkin as shown in Figure 126. Then place the paper dolls on top of the handkerchief.

Instantly the paper dolls come to life, curling and uncurling, twisting and turning on top of the handkerchief. There is an oddly magical quality to the animations of the paper figures.

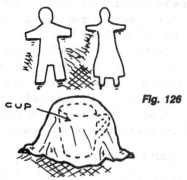

CUP

Fig. 126

You can explain how the movements of the paper dolls relate to future events by pointing out that, by tradition, if the left side moves it means an affair of the heart, while if the right side moves it means affairs of the pocketbook. Thus the movement of the paper figures indicates matters of love or money.

The trick works itself but the reader will have to experiment to find the paper that works best. The feat will work with ordinary bond paper or with glazed paper. Cellophane works well. Cut out the figures from the cellophane wrapper on a cigarette pack. Add human features with a pen. Then drop the figures onto a thin handkerchief or cloth napkin covering the teacup and they will come to life instantly.

If you have a movie or video camera and wish to create offbeat optical effects, Jerry Andrus suggested a clever idea. Cut out the letters spelling "The End" from red cellophane and put them in order on a white cloth handkerchief. Then place the handkerchief over a bowl of steaming water and start the movie camera. The letters will cavort about, twisting and turning in a jumble of movements.

Have the film developed. Then run it backwards through a projector. The magical result is that some highly animated bits of red cellophane are seen to roll and twist about on a white background. Magically they then form themselves into letters which spell "The End."

29 REACHING THROUGH A PLAYING CARD

Bet that in a playing card you can cut a hole large enough to put your arm through. It seems impossible but there is a way to cut an ordinary playing card so that a large hole will be formed.

First cut the card across the middle, almost from end to end, as shown in Figure 127. Then fold the card in half along the middle, Figure 128. Make a number of cuts up to a point almost at the center of the card, Figure 129A, then make a number of cuts down from the top almost to the bottom as in Figure 129B. Note that these cuts alternate with the cuts previously made.

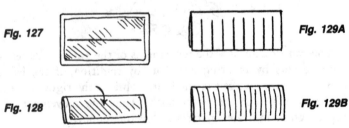

Fig. 127

Fig. 129A

Fig. 128

Fig. 129B

Unfold the card. You will be surprised at how wide a circle it makes when opened out, easily allowing you to put your arm through. If you are slender and agile, you can even step through the opened card.

If this stunt is known to someone in your audience, you can follow it with a completely different version. See Bob Neale's "The Trapdoor" (No. 63) for a new approach to the problem of stepping through a playing card.

30 STRETCHING A DOLLAR BILL

A dollar bill can be cut in such a way that it will seem to stretch between your hands magically, Figure 130. It might seem that this method is the same as the one previously described, but note that the opened playing card can't be easily refolded. The stretching dollar bill opens and closes like an accordion. The method is not well known.

METHOD: Crease the bill along its middle A–B, then unfold the bill. Fold the top quarter C down to the center and the bottom quarter D up to the center, Figure 131.

Fold the bill in half along A–B. The result is shown in Figure 132.

Now cut the bill as indicated in Figure 133. The first cut is made at the far left and is down from the top. The next cut is just to the right of it and is up from the bottom. The next cut is down from the top, the next up from the bottom, and so on. Make the cuts as close together as possible.

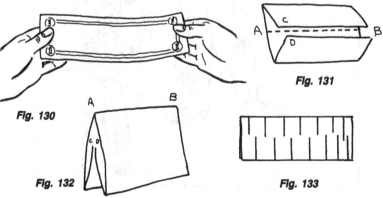

Fig. 130

Fig. 131

Fig. 132

Fig. 133

After cutting, open out the bill. Make sure it is opened out flat. Wet it and leave it under a flat glass surface overnight. A glass cooking pan is ideal for the purpose. The next day the bill will be perfectly flat. Because of the printing on the bill, the cuts will not be noticeable.

To present the stunt, remark that you've figured out a way to stretch your money. Remove the prepared dollar bill from the wallet and stretch it back and forth accordion-style between your hands, Figure 130. It is a startling sight.

Put the bill away before anyone asks to see it.

31 SQUARE DANCE

This delightful paper puzzle appears in Henry Dudeney's scrapbook. It would make an ideal advertising novelty with the puzzle on one side and your advertising message on the other.

Given the 5″ × 5″ square shown in Figure 134, the spectator is to

Fig. 134

cut it in four parts that can be put together to make two squares, each square containg a picture of a clown.

The solution is to cut the square as indicated in Figure 135. Reassemble it as shown in Figure 136 and the solution is complete.

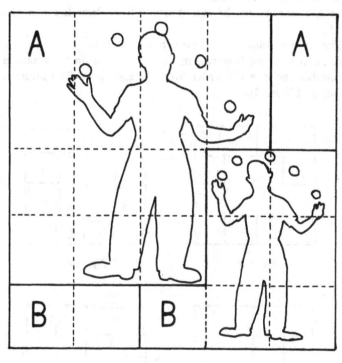

Fig. 135

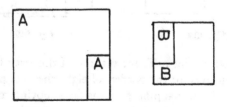

Fig. 136

32 EIGHT SQUARES

This curious puzzle was described by Kobon Fumimure. Eight identical paper squares are placed on top of one another as shown in Figure 137. The top sheet is labeled 1. You are to number the other sheets in order from the top down. In other words, which sheet lies just under the top sheet? Which sheet lies just under that?

The unique solution is shown in Figure 138.

Another example is shown in Figure 139. Again the problem is to number the layers in order from the top down. The solution is shown in Figure 140.

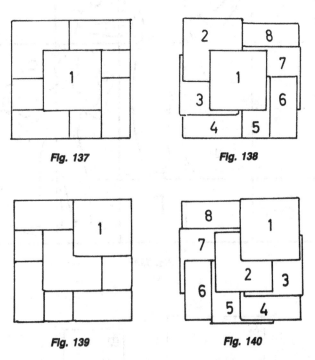

Fig. 137   Fig. 138

Fig. 139   Fig. 140

The reader can invent different versions of this trick for himself. Use a red pencil to color the borders of eight sheets of paper. Then place the sheets in overlapping patterns on a copying machine and take a picture of the result. Ask a friend to determine the order of the sheets from the copy.

33   THE GENIUS TEST

When geniuses fall in love, they take a test to see if they will be compatible. The man gives the lady the apparatus shown in Figure 141. If she can get the wedding bands off the card without tearing the card or cutting the string, it means a successful marriage for the happy couple.

Of course the hole in the playing card is too small for either ring to slide through. How will she get the rings free of the card?

METHOD: The secret is shown at a glance in Figure 142. When constructing the apparatus, make sure the strip in the card is slightly smaller than the width of the hole. The rings should be larger than the hole in the card.

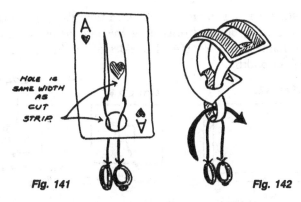

HOLE IS SAME WIDTH AS CUT STRIP.

Fig. 141   **Fig. 142**

To set up the apparatus, bend the top of the card down, then pull the strip through the hole as shown in Figure 142. Thread the rings through the strip, then straighten the apparatus. The result will be the situation of Figure 141.

When the spectator gives up trying to free the rings, put the apparatus out of sight below the level of the table, or turn your back. Then perform the moves of Figure 142 to free the rings.

The following trick is a good encore.

34   THE OTHER GENIUS TEST

When geniuses meet, the lady who wishes to test her prospective mate's compatibility will give him this test. Handed the apparatus of Figure 143, he is to separate all pieces from one another without cutting or tearing. It can be done in a few seconds if he has the right insight.

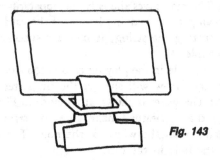

Fig. 143

METHOD: The apparatus is constructed from two playing cards. Begin by cutting out and discarding the interior of one card to form the frame of Figure 144. The sides of the frame should be about ½″ in width.

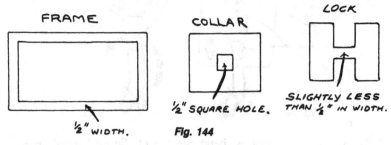

FRAME

COLLAR

LOCK

½″ WIDTH.

½″ SQUARE HOLE.

SLIGHTLY LESS THAN ½″ IN WIDTH.

Fig. 144

The other playing card is cut in half. One half is then used to make the collar. The interior square is about ½″ on a side.

The other half of the playing card is used for the lock. The center part should be just slightly less than ½″ in width. Try to keep the other dimensions as large as possible so that when the lock is in place it can't slip out of the collar.

To set up the apparatus, bend the frame almost in half, Figure 145. Take care not to crease it too tightly because you don't want to break the card. Fold the lock in half and hang it over one side of the frame as shown. Then slip the collar over the top of the frame and slide it around to a position over the lock. Carefully straighten out the apparatus. You will be at the starting position of Figure 143.

Fig. 145

Hand the apparatus to the spectator and ask if it can be solved. Glance at your watch and add, "You should be able to do it in less than a minute." Most people don't work well under pressure. By giving the spectator a time limit you all but guarantee that he won't be able to solve the problem.

35 THE MONEY TREE

The newspaper tree is one of the classic stunts that can be done with newspaper. Although its construction is well known, the method of presenting it is not familiar to most people.

Open out a sheet of newspaper and then roll it snugly into a cylinder as shown in Figure 146. Cut the cylinder in three places equidistant around its circumference. The cuts should extend halfway down the length of the cylinder, Figure 147. Spread the cut pieces and reach into the center of the rolled newspaper, Figure 148.

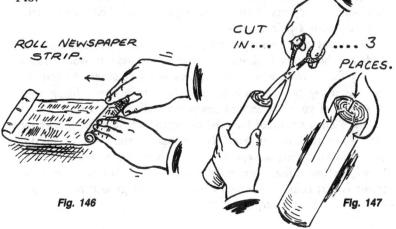

ROLL NEWSPAPER STRIP.

CUT IN... ....3 PLACES.

Fig. 146   *Fig. 147*

Pull out the center. Immediately you have created a tree as shown in Figure 149.

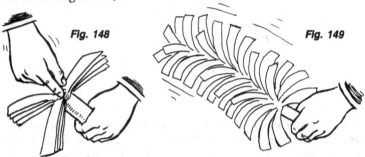

Fig. 148

Fig. 149

The apparatus will be easier to handle if you first cut the newspaper lengthwise and use just half a sheet. To get a newspaper tree tall enough to stretch from floor to ceiling, use four sheets of newspaper. Cut or tear them in half lengthwise and then stack them on top of one another. Roll them up into a cylinder and snap a rubber band around the cylinder to keep it from unrolling.

Make the cuts shown in Figure 147. Then open out the cut pieces as in Figure 148 and begin to pull the center out. Twist the stalk to tighten it after each pull. You will find that the newspaper tree can be made to extend six to eight feet in height.

Different-colored papers can be used to make a tree with colored branches.

To use the newspaper tree in the context of a magic trick it is only necessary to have a handful of change in your pocket. The newspaper used should be one that specializes in business news or stock-market reports. Roll up the paper as described above. Make the cuts with a pair of scissors.

Open out the newspaper tree, all the while explaining to the audience how this business newspaper promised it would make money for its readers. Put the scissors in your pocket. As you do, grab as many coins as you can and close your hand. Bring your hand out of your pocket and grasp the stalk of the tree.

Say, "Then I realized how the newspaper could make money for me. It's really a money tree." Begin shaking the tree. As you do, tilt it down a bit, always keeping it pointing to the audience. Slowly release coins from your hand as it shakes the tree. The result is that coins will scatter about on the stage as if pouring out of the tree. It is a surprising trick.

36 THE MAGIC FLUTE

The magician constructs several simple flutes from paper. Each of the children gathered around the table takes a flute, leaving one for the magician. He blows through the flute and produces a loud noise. When the children try it they find it impossible to make a noise.

When a child gives up, the magician whispers the secret to him. That child is instantly able to make a loud sound with his flute. As the secret is passed around, more and more children are able to create noises with the paper flutes. Adults will be bothered to distraction by the resulting cacophony, but it delights children.

METHOD: Each flute is made from a square of paper. Place a pencil at the bottom corner of a sheet of paper and roll up the paper diagonally, Figure 150. Put tape around the middle, Figure 151, to keep the flute from unraveling. Remove the pencil from inside.

Cut the flute almost all the way around as shown in Figure 152. The result will be that you've created a reed, Figure 153. Fold it down, Figure 154. It must lie flat in order for the flute to work properly.

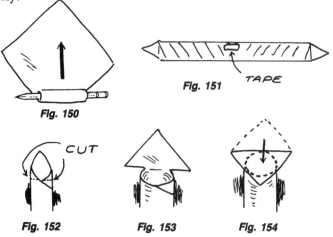

Fig. 150

Fig. 151 TAPE

CUT

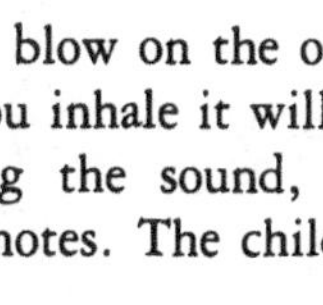

Fig. 152 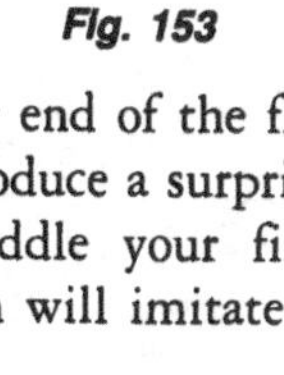   **Fig. 153** 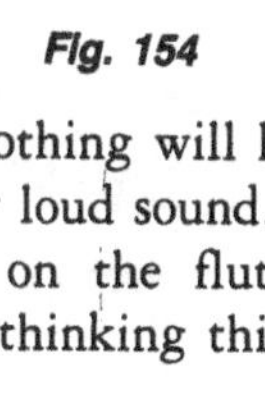   **Fig. 154**

If you blow on the other end of the flute nothing will happen. But if you inhale it will produce a surprisingly loud sound. When producing the sound, twiddle your fingers on the flute as if playing notes. The children will imitate you, thinking this is the secret of producing sounds. Try to make it look as if you are blowing into the tube rather than inhaling.

When a child gives up, whisper the secret to him or her. Do the same with other children in turn. Gradually the room will fill with noise.

Use large squares of paper to make the paper flutes. After they are made, trim the end opposite the reed to produce flutes of different lengths. Then each flute will emit a different pitch. You will probably not be invited back, but the kids will enjoy the noise produced by the paper flutes.

AMAZING ANIMALS

Animals can do tricks as well as people. The paper animals in this chapter are easy to make and seem to have personalities of their own. In addition they appear to have the uncanny ability to come to life and perform magic tricks.

37 RUPERT THE GREAT

This is a novel way to find a chosen card. Besides the use of any borrowed deck of cards, you will need only an envelope and a pair of scissors. A creature named Rupert is made from the envelope. He then finds a chosen card in a novel way.

METHOD: If you use a fresh envelope to construct Rupert, begin by sealing the flap. Then trim the ends so you have a paper tube, Figure 155. Now cut a slit from right to left about 1″ from the top. Cut to within ½″ of the left side of the envelope. Make another slit about 1″ up from the bottom, but cut it from left to right. The slits are indicated by the arrows in Figure 156.

Add an eye on either side in the position shown. Trim away ¼″ at the bottom left corner, Figure 157. This completes the scissor work. You will now open out the model as follows.

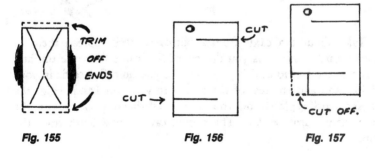

Fig. 155   Fig. 156   Fig. 157

Grasp the envelope at the left side. With your right forefinger push in the crease at the right side of the envelope, Figure 158. As indicated in Figure 158, as the crease is pushed in, the legs at the bottom will automatically swing around toward the right side. When the crease has been pushed all the way to the left the result will be the cartoonlike character of Figure 159. This completes the construction of Rupert.

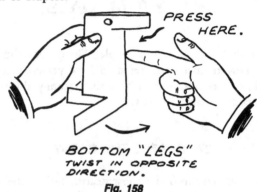

Fig. 158

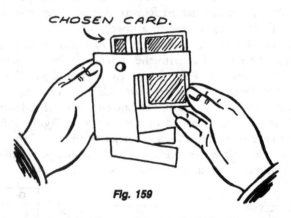

Fig. 159

Take about ten cards from a borrowed deck. Spread them to have a card chosen. As you do, count five cards from the top and separate the spread at this point so that you hold five cards in your right hand and the rest of the packet in your left hand. Have the chosen card replaced on top of the left-hand packet. Put the right-hand cards on top. The chosen card is now sixth from the top.

Explain that Rupert is a nervous but gifted magician who will try to find the chosen card. As you talk, take the top two cards of the packet and transfer them to the bottom. Transfer two more cards, then two more for a total of six. The chosen card is now at the bottom of the packet.

Holding Rupert in your left hand and the packet in your right hand, slip the packet between the folds of Rupert's beak, Figure 159. Note in Figure 159 that the chosen card on the bottom of the packet is spread slightly away from the rest of the packet. This is to allow the chosen card to be gripped firmly between your left thumb and forefinger. The other cards are held in place by pressure of your left fingers.

Remark that Rupert gets nervous when asked to perform. Shake the apparatus up and down, gradually making the shaking more animated. As you do, allow your fingers to release pressure. The result is that cards will fly through the air, some propelled over Rupert's head, some down through his legs. Continue until only the chosen card remains.

Have the chosen card named. Then remove it from Rupert's beak and show it to the audience.

This routine was devised by the author. Another method of presentation is to mail yourself an empty sealed envelope. Bring it with you to the performance. Explain that a magical mail-order house sent you this envelope, advertising it would find any card chosen by the audience. Trim away the ends, saying you were puzzled because the envelope was clearly empty. As you talk, make the necessary cuts and form Rupert. When the figure is complete, say, "I've gotten many magic tricks in the mail but this is the first time that the envelope was the trick." Proceed from here with the routine as written above. Instead of transferring cards from top to bottom as described, you can spell R-U-P-E-R-T, transferring one card from top to bottom for each letter.

38 HUNGRY DOG

A piece of paper is folded. The magician sketches a dog on it. Holding aloft a picture of a bone, the magician asks the dog to sit up. The dog springs to life and stands straight up.

METHOD: This trick was originally published by Eric Kenneway. The fold is of Japanese origin.

Use a square of thin, springy paper. A sheet measuring about 8″ on a side is about right.

The paper is aligned as shown in Figure 160. Make the center diagonal crease from top to bottom. Open up the paper. The result will be the solid crease shown in Figure 160.

Again referring to Figure 160, fold the right and left corners in to the center crease, following the arrows in Figure 160. The result is shown in Figure 161.

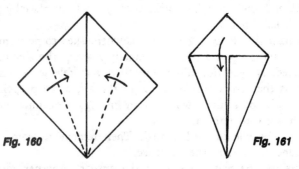

Fig. 160   Fig. 161

Now fold the top point down as indicated by the arrow in Figure 161. Fold the top corners down so they lie on either side of the center vertical crease in Figure 162. The result is shown in Figure 163. Fold the top point down in the direction indicated by the arrow in Figure 163.

Fold the top corners down once more in the direction of the arrows in Figure 164 so the corners line up on either side of the center line.

Fig. 162   Fig. 163   Fig. 164

Finally, fold the model in half as indicated in Figure 165. Place it on a flat surface and it will slowly come to life and tip up to a vertical position as indicated in Figure 166. At times it will stand up and then tip over.

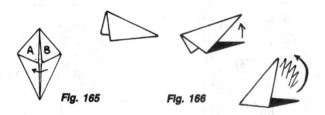

Fig. 165   Fig. 166

If the model tips up too quickly, it probably needs a firmer crease at the spine. If it does not move at all, make sure that the flaps A and B are pushing against each other inside the model. A slight realignment of the flaps is sometimes needed to allow this to take place.

Martin Gardner suggested sketching a dog on the sides of the model as in Figure 167. Draw a picture of a bone on a piece of paper and say something like, "Here Fido; sit up!" The dog obediently springs to life.

Fig. 167

39 HOUDINI HOUND

This is a funny way to locate a chosen card. The card, chosen from an ordinary deck, is signed by the spectator. The deck is put aside. Then the magician introduces Houdini Hound, a goofy-looking dog constructed from a paper bag, Figure 168.

The dog is offered a cardboard bone so that he will be encouraged to find the selected card. Instantly and in full sight, the bone changes to the signed chosen card.

Kids are amazed at the sight of the dog, but adults will be surprised and baffled at the way the dog finds the chosen card.

METHOD: The dog is constructed from an ordinary brown paper bag. The eyes, nose, ears and other features are cut from white paper, glued onto the bag and colored with crayon. The features can also be made from brightly colored construction paper.

The bag should be large enough to fit comfortably over the arm puppet-style, as shown in Figure 169. A slit is cut into the bag. The slit should be wide enough for a playing card to slide through.

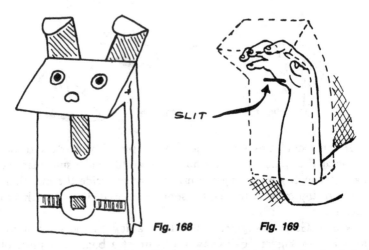

Fig. 168   **Fig. 169**

The slit should be hidden from audience view when the dog's jaw is lowered to the position of Figure 168.

The only other major preparation regarding the dog is to cut a hole in the back of the bag, Figure 170. The hole should be large enough for your hand to fit through. The back of the bag is never shown to the audience.

Also required is a bone made from blank white cardboard. The cardboard is exactly the size of a playing card. Cut away the excess, Figure 171, to produce the proper shape. If white cardboard isn't available, you can cut a panel from a cardboard box, then cover it with white paper to produce the same result.

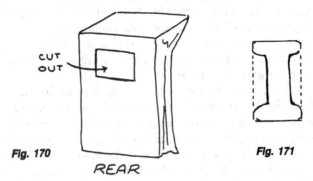

Fig. 170   **Fig. 171**

The cardboard bone is on the bottom of the deck. The ♣A is on top of the deck. This completes the preparation.

Tell your audience that you've spent years training household pets to do card tricks. You are about to introduce your latest marvel. To do so, you will have someone pick a card.

Go to the nearest spectator and give him the top card (♣A) along with a pencil. Tell him to sign his name on the face of the card. When he's done this, take back the signed card and place it on top of the deck. Cut the deck and complete the cut. This brings the cardboard bone directly on top of the chosen card.

Go back to the table where the paper bag is. Say, "To encourage this amazing animal to find your card, I feed him a bone." Spread the cards until you spot the cardboard bone. Cut the deck at that point and complete the cut. Unknown to the audience the signed card is now on top of the deck. Toss the cardboard bone onto the table.

The handling from here is important because it sets up the surprise finish. Your left hand holds the deck. Your left second, third and fourth fingers slip over the top of the bag so the bag is clipped between these fingers and your forefinger, Figure 172.

Lift the bag so the audience can see the front. At the same time slip your right hand inside the bag. Your right hand reaches through the opening in back of the bag and takes the top card of the deck, Figure 173. This is the chosen card. Your left hand remains stationary while your right hand takes the chosen card. The action is concealed from audience view by the bag itself.

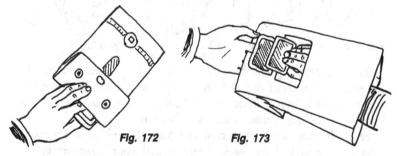

Fig. 172   Fig. 173

When your right hand has a firm grasp on the chosen card, slip your right hand back inside the bag. Pause for a moment. Say to the audience, "Do you know what this is?" Wait for someone to offer a guess. Then say, "A doggie bag."

Put the deck on the table. If you have a small paper bag on the table, pick it up and say, "Here's what he looked like when he was young." Put the small bag down.

Your left hand now grasps the bag in the vicinity of the dog's jaw as if to make a slight adjustment. While your left hand holds the bag your right hand, inside the bag, guides the ♣A, face outward, into the slit in front. An exposed view is shown in Figure 174. To avoid fumbling at this crucial point, note that you can see into the bag through the window in back, so it is easy to guide the ♣A into the slot since the action is visible to you.

To cover any hesitation, you can make jokes that relate to the paper bags. For instance, you can say, "We call him Houdini Hound although I doubt he could find his way out of a paper bag. On Halloween he disguises himself as a shopping bag."

Pick up the cardboard bone. Slide it into the slit under the jaw, Figure 175A. The cardboard bone is taken by your right hand. At the same time, the ♣A is taken by your left hand. As soon as this exchange takes place, draw the ♣A down so its lower quarter is visible to the audience, Figure 175B.

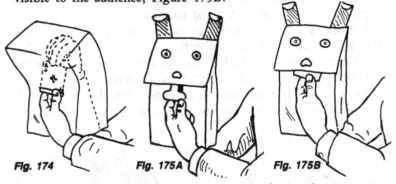

Fig. 174   Fig. 175A   Fig. 175B

The important point here is that your left thumb covers the lower index corner of the ♣A, so it appears as if this card is really the cardboard bone. From the audience's view you inserted the bone into the dog's mouth and still hold it.

Say, "By the way, what card did you choose?" The spectator tells you he picked the ♣A. "And it had your signature on it, right?" The spectator has to agree.

Turn to the dog. "I say the magic words 'Fetch, boy,' and here's what he does."

Slowly draw the ♣A down into view. It appears as if the cardboard bone visibly and instantly changed to a playing card. Have the spectator verify his signature. Let Houdini Hound take all the bows.

40 THE SHADOW

Shadowgraphs were once a popular form of entertainment. Placing his hands behind a translucent screen illuminated by a strong light, the vaudeville performer created a surprising array of animated figures. I wanted a close-up version of shadowgraphs with a bit of magic thrown in. The following routine was devised for this purpose.

The magician shows a cutout of a dog, Figure 176. He points out that the dog is asleep because its eyes are closed. The dog wakes up only when it's time for supper.

The cutout is slipped into an envelope and the envelope is sealed. It is held up to the light so the audience can see the shadow of the sleeping dog. The magician then says, "Time for supper," and, magically, the dog wakes up and opens its eyes.

The spectator himself may open the envelope and remove the cutout. He will find that the dog's eyes are indeed open.

METHOD: There are really two dogs: the sleeping dog of Figure 176 and the wide-awake dog of Figure 177. One is switched for the other by the method described in "Deluxe Headline Reading" (No. 21).

Fig. 176   **Fig. 177**

Begin with a stack of envelopes. Use thin envelopes that allow the light to shine through. Place the wide-awake dog in the top envelope. Then remove the flap from another envelope as in Figure 110 and place it on top of all. Snap a rubber band around the package of envelopes. The situation is as shown in Figure 178.

Show the audience the sleeping dog of Figure 176. Let them look it over to satisfy themselves that it is nothing more than a cardboard cutout free of any gimmickry.

Remove the stack of envelopes from the pocket. Place the sleeping dog into the first envelope. Unknown to the audience this is really the flapless envelope. Grasp the flap of the next envelope (the one containing the wide-awake dog) and pull this envelope free of the stack. Seal the envelope and hold it up to the light in the following way.

The envelope has to be grasped as in Figure 179, clipped between your first and second fingers. An exposed view of the back of the envelope is shown in Figure 180. This is the key to the method. Your third finger is directly over the dog's eye, blocking out the light. This means that when the envelope is held up to the light, it appears as if the dog's eye is still closed.

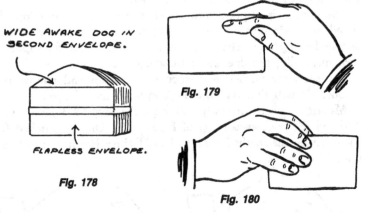

WIDE AWAKE DOG IN
SECOND ENVELOPE.

FLAPLESS ENVELOPE.

Fig. 178

Fig. 179

Fig. 180

Say the magic words, "Time for supper!" Pause here to focus audience attention. Repeat the magic words. Pause again. Then repeat the words once more. Slowly draw away your third finger. The dog's eye opens magically.

Hand the envelope to a spectator. Let him open it and remove the dog to prove that the dog did indeed wake up for supper.

The best way to construct the apparatus is to begin at the end. Take an empty envelope and hold it up to the light as shown in Figure 179. With a pencil trace the position of your third finger when it is extended behind the envelope. This will tell you how far your third finger can comfortably travel to block off the dog's eyes. Draw a circle for the eye. Then sketch in the rest of the figure on the face of the envelope. Use this as a template when you cut out the two dogs from cardboard or black construction paper.

Depending on your digital agility you can construct a duck whose bill moves, a cartoon figure whose nose shrinks when it tells the truth or a jack-o'-lantern whose mouth opens when you whisper to it the name of a chosen card.

41 SNAPPER

The spectator is given three slips of paper. He is asked to write his true weight on one slip and false weights on the others. The three slips are then loosely crumpled up and placed on the table.

The magician shows a folded piece of paper that loosely resembles a duck. Introducing the duck as Snapper, the magician explains that Snapper has been educated to guess the spectator's weight.

The duck looks at the spectator as if gauging his weight. Then the duck opens and closes his bill, blowing away two of the slips of paper. The remaining slip is unfolded. It is the one that contains the spectator's correct weight.

METHOD: There are two tricks here. The first is the means of knowing which slip contains the spectator's weight. This method was invented by Henry Hardin.

Tear a piece of paper into three pieces, Figure 181. Give the center section to the spectator and have him jot down his correct weight. Then have him jot down incorrect weights on the other two pieces. He wads up each piece of paper. The pieces are mixed and placed on the table.

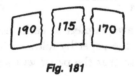

Fig. 181

The way to determine which slip contains the correct weight is to note that the center section contains two ragged edges, Figure 181. These are the uneven edges formed when the paper was torn. Each of the other segments contains one ragged edge. By this simple means you know which segment contains the correct weight; simply look for the segment that has two ragged edges.

The educated duck is made from a square of paper measuring about 8½" on each side. Fold the paper in half, Figure 182. Then fold the front layer of B–B up along the dotted line so that it meets A–A. Turn the paper over side for side (left to right) and fold B–B up to meet A–A. The result is shown in Figure 183. The paper resembles the letter W.

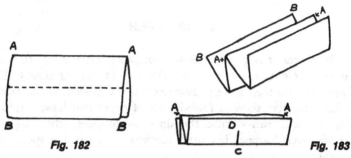

Fig. 182   Fig. 183

With a pair of scissors cut slot C–D through all four thicknesses at the center of the paper up to about midpoint, Figure 183. At the left side fold down three thicknesses as shown in Figure 184. Repeat with three thicknesses at the right side.

Turn the paper over side for side and fold over the one remaining thickness at the left. Then fold over the one remaining thickness at the right. The situation now is shown in Figure 185. Make an eye on the side of the paper as indicated in Figure 185.

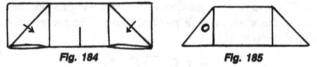

Fig. 184   Fig. 185

With scissors, trim away a piece at each end, Figure 186. Then turn up the bottom of the paper by folding along the dotted line. Do this on both sides so that the paper will look like Figure 187.

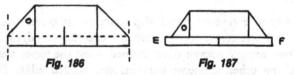

Fig. 186   Fig. 187

If E and F are brought together, you will get the duck of Figure 188. Hold the duck as in Figure 189. Pressure from your thumb and forefinger, coupled with the natural springiness of the paper, will cause the duck to open and close his mouth with a loud snap.

To return to the trick, when the loosely crumpled pieces of

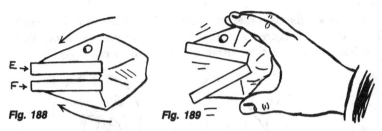

Fig. 188   Fig. 189

paper are on the table, note which one contains the two ragged edges. This is the paper with the spectator's correct weight. Have the duck stare at the spectator as if mentally gauging his weight. If you can make duck sounds, you can have the duck make comments about the spectator's physical condition.

Point the duck toward the slips of paper. As you open and close his bill next to each slip, secretly blow the unwanted slips away. Properly timed, it appears that the duck is doing it.

You're left with one slip. Ask the spectator for his correct weight. Then have that slip opened. The educated duck guessed the spectator's weight correctly.

42 RABBIT EARS

Animated paper folds such as the classic flapping bird are a source of fascination. Most are outside the scope of this book because many intricate folds are required. Jack Chanin devised a charming paper rabbit that flaps its ears. The rabbit can be made in a few seconds. It is simple enough for anyone to learn.

Begin with a square of paper measuring about 4" on each side. Fold up the bottom half along the dotted line shown in Figure 190. The result is the triangle shown in Figure 191. Add eyes and a mouth. Then tear along the dotted line of Figure 191.

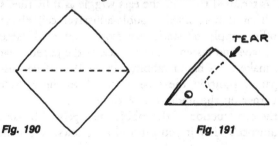

Fig. 190   Fig. 191

Fold down the flaps that were formed by the last tear. The result is the rabbit of Figure 192. Hold the rabbit in your left hand. Pull the flaps with your right hand and the rabbit's ears wiggle.

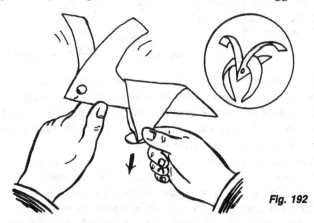

Fig. 192

The rabbit's ears can be curled outward, the left ear to the left, the right ear to the right. This gives them a bit more shape. Experiment with squares of different sizes to find the one that you feel the most comfortable with. The tear of Figure 191 can be varied to produce ears of different shapes. A method of causing the rabbit's ears to wiggle as if by themselves is described next.

43   THE EDUCATED RABBIT

A paper rabbit is perched on top of a drinking cup. When someone asks it a question, the rabbit mysteriously flaps its ears, one wiggle for yes, two for no.

The basic design is the Chanin rabbit. Some slight additional preparation is required to make the ears wiggle as if by themselves. Secure a roll of double-sided (double-adhesive) cellophane tape from any office-supply or stationery store. Cut a ¼″ square of double-sided tape and fasten it to the back of the paper square you will use to make the Chanin rabbit, Figure 193. If you use a 4″ square of paper, position the tape about 1″ to the right of the upper left corner on the underside of the paper.

During the construction of the rabbit the tape will be concealed from the audience's view if you proceed as follows. With the tape on the underside as in Figure 193, fold the bottom half up to the position of Figure 191. Make the tear as indicated and bring the flaps down as in Figure 192. Press tightly, causing the flaps to adhere together, Figure 194, to form a ring.

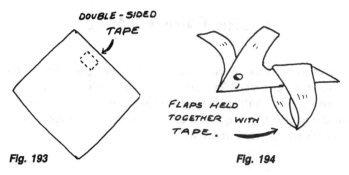

Fig. 193   **Fig. 194**

The only other requirement is a paper cup that has a hole cut from it, Figure 195. Place the paper rabbit on top of the cup. Grasp the cup between your thumb and middle finger. Your forefinger goes through the hole in the cup and slips into the ring formed by the taped-together flaps, Figure 196.

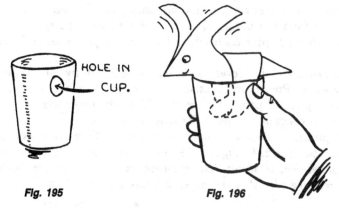

Fig. 195   **Fig. 196**

By moving your forefinger up and down, the rabbit's ears will mysteriously flap. To incorporate this into a magic trick, ask a child to pick a jelly bean of a particular color from among an assortment. Say the child picks blue. Put several jelly beans in a row on the table. Position the rabbit in front of each one. When the rabbit gets to the blue jelly bean, its ears wiggle.

MORE PAPER MAGIC

Some of the tricks in this chapter were designed for close-up performance. Others, like "Sprightly Soda" (No. 48) and "Spot Remover" (No. 54), are showy enough in effect to be done from the platform or stage. All of the tricks in this chapter provide strong visual magic at its best.

44 DOUBLE CROSS

A piece of paper is torn in half, then in half again and then in half once more to form eight pieces. Four of the pieces are given to the spectator to hold in his hand. The performer draws an X on each of the other four pieces.

These four pieces are put into an ashtray and burned. Some of the ashes from the burnt paper are sprinkled over the spectator's hand. When he opens his hand, each of the four pieces has an X on it.

METHOD: This clever trick was originated by Milbourne Christopher. Preparation consists of drawing X's in the left-hand half of a piece of paper, Figure 197. Turn the paper over so the writing is concealed. This is the only preparation.

To present the trick, remove the paper so the writing side is down. Tear it in half, Figure 198, and place B under A. Turn the two pieces over as a unit. The audience sees a blank surface. This reinforces the idea that the paper is blank on both sides.

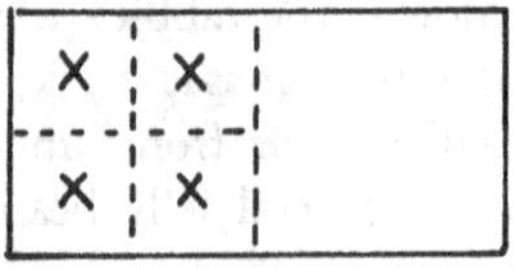

Fig. 197 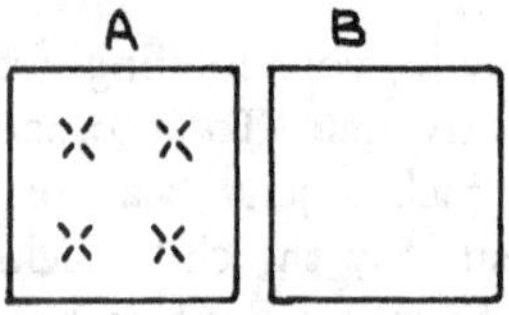   Fig. 198

Tear the paper in half again, Figure 199. Place D behind (in back of) C. Tear in half again, Figure 200. Place F behind E. Turn the packet over.

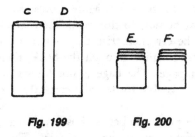

Fig. 199   **Fig. 200**

Deal the torn pieces one at a time into two piles on the table, alternating left to right as you deal. All of the blank pieces will be in one pile. All of the prepared pieces will be in the other pile. Place the prepared pile in the spectator's hand. Have him close his hand.

On each of the remaining pieces draw an X. Crumple them, drop them into an ashtray and set them on fire. When they have burned completely, sprinkle some of the ashes onto the spectator's hand. He opens his hand and discovers the X's are now on the pieces he holds.

If you can find out the name of one of the spectators you intend to do the trick for, someone you do not know personally, then beforehand you can jot down his name in the prepared squares instead of the X's shown in Figure 197. When ready to do the trick, tear the paper as described above. Then put the four blank pieces on the table in the form of a square and pretend you are going to fill them in with random designs. Then, almost as a seeming afterthought, ask the spectator for his name and fill it in on the blank squares. It appears as if you found out his name at just that minute.

Proceed with the rest of the trick, burning the papers and then having the spectator open his hand to discover his name on the other papers. Performed this way it appears that a name you did not previously know was caused to migrate from one place to another.

The handling should be done exactly as described above. The tearing and turning over of the paper appears casual and gives the impression that the paper is blank on both sides.

45 MURDER BY MEMORY

The magician goes to a friend's home and asks the friend to choose a book from his bookcase. Murder mysteries are popular and are found in most homes, so this would be a good selection. The magician claims he can memorize the content of the book in less than five minutes. He flips through the book, then has the friend choose a random page. The page is not known by the magician beforehand, yet he is able to describe correctly the content of the chosen page.

METHOD: The page number is chosen in such a way that only one of a few different pages can be chosen. Thus when flipping through the book to memorize the content, you really look at only four different pages.

To set up the number force, have six blank slips in a stack. On the top slip write 1, turn the slip writing-side down and place it on the table. On the next slip write 2, turn it writing-side down and place it on top of the no. 1 slip. Number the next slip 3, turn it writing-side down and place it on top of the no. 2 slip. Proceed in the same way with the remaining slips, numbering them 4, 5 and 6 respectively and placing each writing-side down on top of the other slips.

On the blank uppermost side of the top slip write the number 7 and place this slip on the table with the 7 side up. The number 6 is on the underside of this slip. On the next slip write 8. Place this slip on top of the 7 slip with the 8 side uppermost. On the next slip write 9 and place this slip on top of the no. 8 slip with the 9 side uppermost. Proceed in the same way with the remaining slips, numbering them 10, 11 and 12 respectively and placing each on top of the previous slip. The no. 12 slip should have the number 1 on the underside. The no. 11 slip should have the number 2 on the underside and so on. Keep the slips in numerical order.

Hand the packet of slips to a spectator. While you pretend to memorize the paperback book he's given you, have him turn over the packet of slips several times. He then cuts the packet several times.

After the final cut he notes the number on top of the packet. Say it is 4. He deals four slips one at a time from top to bottom. Whatever number now shows on top, he removes that slip, turns it over and places it on the table. In our example the slip will bear the number 6. He turns it over, bringing the number 7 uppermost, and places the slip on the table.

The spectator turns over the packet and gives it several random cuts. He notes the number on top and transfers that many slips from top to bottom. If, for example, the number on top is 9, he would transfer 9 slips from top to bottom. This brings the no. 10 slip to the top. He turns it over and places it on the table. The uppermost number on this slip is 3.

The chosen slips bear the numbers 3 and 7. The spectator can open the book to page 37 or page 73. The choice is his. Unknown to him, this is one of four force numbers. The spectator can arrive at page 37, 73, 18 or 81. No other result is possible.

You have familiarized yourself with the content of these four pages in the book handed to you. When he announces his choice, pretend to concentrate, then reveal the general information about the chosen page.

Since so few pages are involved, it isn't necessary for him to announce the chosen page number. You can remark that you see a mental picture of a beautiful blond or a cigar-chomping hitman. The spectator opens the book to the chosen page and checks to see whether you're right. Even if you are not correct, it is a simple matter to describe the content of the other pages you looked at and slowly narrow in on the correct page.

46 TAKE A VACATION

The magician exhibits a number of file cards. On each is the name of a city, a geometric symbol or the picture of a playing card. The cards are shown to contain different information. Then the cards are tossed into a paper bag.

A spectator in the audience shakes up the contents of the bag, reaches in and removes a card. He notes what it says, then drops it back into the bag. The bag is passed to a second spectator who shakes the contents of the bag, reaches in and removes a card. When he's noted what's on the card, he tosses the card back into the bag.

A third spectator likewise shakes up the bag, reaches in and chooses any file card. He notes the content, then tosses the file card back into the bag.

The magician, standing some distance away, draws something on each of three pieces of cardboard. When his drawings are shown, they prove to match correctly the file cards chosen by the spectators. Only one group of file cards is used. Nothing is switched. The bag is ordinary. The cards are not marked.

METHOD: Each of the cards has the word "Paris" written on it. Write the word "Paris" in large letters on some cards, in small letters on others. Use crayon for some of the cards, marking pens for others. Write in different colors and in different styles.

On three other cards draw a picture of the ♣2, a picture of a triangle and the word "Rome." These three cards are placed on the face of the packet of file cards.

Display the cards by showing the ♣2 card and transferring it to the back of the packet. Then display the triangle card and transfer it to the back of the packet. Then riffle the ends of the remaining cards to show that all are apparently different.

Place the packet of file cards into the paper bag. Then remark that you need something to write on. Reach into the bag and apparently remove three random cards. You actually remove the ♣2 card, the triangle card and the Rome card. Now the bag contains only Paris cards.

Have each of three people reach into the bag, mix the contents and remove a card. Each spectator sees the word "Paris." Since the spectators are in widely different parts of the audience, they are not aware that they all chose the same word.

Use the blank sides of the three cards in your possession to draw pictures of the chosen cards. On one card draw a picture of the ♥3. On another draw a circle. On the third write the word "Paris" in large letters.

Don't make the trick look too easy. Go back to the circle card and cross it out. Draw a square. Then hesitate as if unsure. Ask if someone in the auudience who is not a participating spectator is sending you thought waves of a circle. Almost always you will see several hands go up. Say, "I thought so," and cross out the square. Hesitate again, then draw a star. It means nothing since none of the participating spectators chose a geometric symbol, but since you focus attention on the symbol, it appears to be important.

Remark that you think you have all three selections. Show the file card with the ♥3 first, then the file card with the star and finally the file card with the word "Paris." Ask all three of the participating spectators if they saw their selections. They will say yes. Thank them and take your bow.

47   ANIMAL CRACKERS

"When I was a boy," the magician says, "I loved to eat crackers. When the box was empty, this is what I did for a refill."

The spectator is invited to stand alongside the magician. The magician removes two paper napkins from an empty cracker box and gives them to the spectator. The spectator rolls up each napkin and places it on the magician's outstretched palm. The magician taps the empty cracker box against the napkin and then puts the napkin into the box.

When both napkins are inside the empty box, the lid is closed for a moment and then is opened. The napkins are removed. One is unchanged. But when the second napkin is opened, it contains a dozen crackers.

METHOD: Beforehand, put a dozen or so animal crackers or other small crackers into a napkin. Roll up the napkin and put it into the empty cracker box. Put two unprepared napkins into the box as well.

Stand with your right side to the spectator. Hold the box in your right hand so that the side with the lid is toward him, Figure 201. The lid acts as a screen to prevent the spectator from looking into the box.

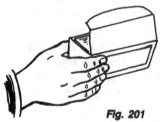

Fig. 201

Remove the two unprepared napkins and hand them to the spectator. Ask him to roll up one napkin into a ball. Extend your left hand palm up and have him place the napkin onto your palm, Figure 202.

Tap the cracker box against the rolled-up napkin as you say, "We'll just tighten it up a bit more."

Then drop the napkin into the box.

Have the spectator roll up the other napkin into a ball. He then places it onto your left palm. As you tap the cracker box against this napkin, allow the other rolled-up napkin to fall out of the box behind the spectator, Figure 203. Squeeze the box as you do this to prevent the prepared napkin from falling out.

Fig. 202   **Fig. 203**

Drop the second napkin into the box and close the lid. Shake the box. Then have the spectator open it. There are still two napkins in the box, but one of them is filled with crackers. The spectator opens the unprepared napkin first. Then he opens the other napkin and finds it filled with crackers.

As to the disposal of the unwanted napkin in Figure 203, if working with a confederate simply have the confederate stand behind you to catch the napkin. If working alone, endeavor to stand near a couch so that the napkin will fly out and land silently behind the couch. When circumstances permit, stand with your back to an open window and let the napkin fly out the window.

For the trick to be successful your arm motions should be exactly the same when genuinely tapping the box against the first napkin as when getting rid of this napkin in Figure 203. If there are others in the room when you do the trick, they will be amused at the assisting spectator's bafflement.

48 SPRIGHTLY SODA

A cup of soda is placed inside a paper bag. It vanishes immediately and appears inside a borrowed hat. This trick, based on a clever routine of Sam Berland's, can be used either as a close-up routine or as a platform trick.

METHOD: Required are two drinking cups. Trim the rolled top from one cup. Then place the other cup into it so the two nest together, Figure 204. The apparatus looks like a single cup.

Borrow a hat and a paper bag. Place the double cup inside the hat. Immediately lift out the top cup as you say, "I'm going to put this cup into the bag. To add weight, let's fill it with soda."

The cup is placed back into the hat, in back of the other cup, and is filled with soda. Then call attention to the paper bag. Let the audience examine it to verify that it's ordinary. Open the bag and put it mouth-up on the table.

Pretend to remove the cup of soda from the hat. Really remove the empty cup and place it into the bag.

As soon as it's out of sight inside the bag, silently crumple the cup. Your left hand gathers the neck of the bag. As it does, grasp the crumpled cup through the bag with your left hand. Remove your right hand from the bag. The crumpled cup is now at the top of the bag, held in place by your left hand as shown in Figure 205.

Smash the bag against the tabletop. It will burst. Tear open the bottom of the bag to show that the cup of soda has completely vanished. Then remove the cup of soda from the hat.

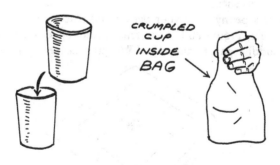

CRUMPLED
CUP
INSIDE
BAG

Fig. 204   **Fig. 205**

49 THE BUDDHA PAPERS

This is a deceptive method of causing a coin or other small flat object to vanish. We will describe the classic method first, then a recent improvement.

You will need two pieces of plain white paper measuring about 9″ on a side. Fold each in thirds so that each square of paper is divided into nine smaller squares. Open both papers.

Place one paper squarely on top of the other. Then glue the center square of the top sheet to the center square of the bottom sheet. The glued squares are shown shaded in Figure 206.

When the glue has dried, fold the top sheet so it forms a package that is 3″ on a side. Then turn over the apparatus and fold the bottom paper so it forms a similar package. Place this on top of a 10″-square piece of newspaper, Figure 207, and fold the newspaper around the package. You now have completed the advance preparation.

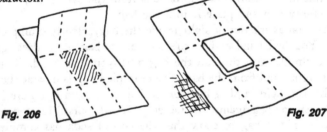

Fig. 206   *Fig. 207*

To present a sample trick, remove the apparatus from your pocket. Unfold the newspaper. Then unfold the top sheet of the Buddha papers. Unknown to the audience there is a folded paper under the top sheet.

Remove a penny from your pocket and place it in the center of the top sheet, Figure 208. Then fold up the top sheet. Pick up the folded Buddha papers and say, "We put the penny here for the

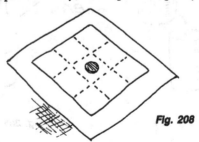

Fig. 208

moment." As you replace the folded Buddha papers on top of the newspaper, turn over the package. Then wrap it in the newspaper.

Say, "Where I live, when you want to take out a classified ad in a newspaper, this is how you pay for the ad." Snap the fingers. Unfold the newspaper. Then unfold the top sheet of the Buddha papers. When you do, it is seen that the penny has vanished.

50 IMPROVED BUDDHA PAPERS

This versatile method of handling the Buddha papers allows you to perform a wide variety of tricks. In the one we will describe here, the magician displays the index corners cut from several playing cards, Figure 209. The spectator has a free choice of any index. Note that all the indexes are from black cards.

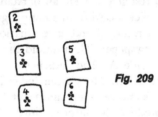

Fig. 209

All five are then wrapped in paper. When the paper is unwrapped, it is seen that the chosen index is face up. All the others are face down. When the others are turned over, they have all changed to red cards.

METHOD: The Buddha papers are modified by cutting a slit right through them, Figure 210. Cut the index corner from each of four red cards. Arrange them all face down and wrap them in the top paper. We will call this side of the Buddha papers side A. Turn over the apparatus. Cut the index corners from five black cards and place them onto the top sheet. Fold up this sheet. We will call this side of the Buddha papers side B. Place the apparatus in your pocket until ready to perform.

To do the trick, open side B, the side that contains the black index corners. Toss them onto the table. Have the spectator select one. Emphasize the freedom of choice. Place this index plus the others onto the open paper, but secretly pass the chosen index face down through the slit, Figure 211. In this way the chosen index is loaded into side A, the compartment that contains the red index corners.

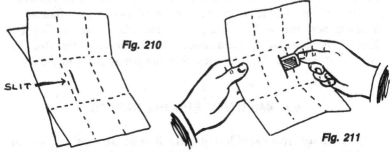

Fig. 210

SLIT →

Fig. 211

The paper itself helps screen the action from the spectator's view. Fold up the paper. Secretly turn over the package as you wrap it in the newspaper. Remark that you saw an ad in the paper that offered to test if you were an outstanding individual. In this test you would pick a card from among a group mailed to you. The cards were then returned and an evaluation was made.

Unfold the newspaper. Then unfold the top sheet of the Buddha papers. This is side A. The audience sees that four of the index corners are face down. The chosen index is face up. Say, "As you can see, you're someone who stands out from the crowd."

You then produce the surprise finish. "You really stand out," you remark as you turn over the four face-down indexes to show that the spectator's choice is the only black index. All the others have changed to red.

Other small objects can be used, including postage stamps, coins, dollar bills and small envelopes. To hide the slit in the Buddha papers, use paper with writing on it. Newsprint is ideal for this purpose, but you can also choose pages from magazines or advertising brochures.

51   THE LESSON

The magician Al Baker taught this trick as a lesson in how to get something for nothing. It is an offhand effect that you can do whenever the occasion presents itself. You need a mantel, shelf or some other place where objects can be placed above your head.

Remove two articles from a newspaper. One might be a story about a fellow who just won the lottery. The other might be a story of a team that just won a major sporting event. Fold up each article. Place them on the mantel or bookshelf about 30″ apart. Have a spectator stand facing them. Ask him to look at them for a minute.

He is to decide upon one of them while your back is turned, take it down, read the headline and then replace it. When this has been done, you turn around, look intently at the spectator, and then tell him the headline he just read!

METHOD: The trick is based on a classic principle but here it is well disguised. When reaching for the news article, the spectator must reach up to the shelf. In the act of doing this, the flow of blood to the hand will slow down. The result will be that this hand is paler than the other. You can try it right now. Simply raise one hand, then lower it. You will find that is is a bit paler than the other hand.

The spectator takes down one news article, reads the headline to himself and then replaces it on the shelf. When this is done he signals the magician, who turns around and glances at the backs of the spectator's hands. He knows immediately which hand was used to get the news article.

The rest is presentation. Explain that you will try to guess whether the spectator is the sort of fellow who would prefer to read about the lottery or about a sports event. Look at him intently. Then reveal which article he chose.

52 DARKROOM EFFECT

The magician opens a paper napkin and cuts a 2″ hole in the center. Then he slips the napkin around the leg of the table by lifting the table leg and guiding it through the hole in the center of the napkin.

Someone is now asked to sit on the table. All others in the group take their places around the table and place their fingertips on the edge of the table.

Clearly the napkin can't be removed from the table leg without first lifting the table leg from the floor. If this were to happen, one of those present will easily detect the movement of the table. Also, the presence of someone sitting on the table makes any secret movement of the table nearly impossible.

The room lights are extinguished for a moment. When they are turned on again, not only is the napkin free of the table leg, but now it is on *another* table leg!

The napkin is ordinary and may be examined before and after.

METHOD: There are really two napkins. To prepare, tear a hole in the center of one, then slip it up onto a table leg. Push it up near the top and tuck it under the table. Take care to do this without tearing the napkin.

A hole is torn in a duplicate napkin. Then you openly lift another table leg and guide it through the hole in this napkin. Slide the napkin up to the midpoint of this table leg.

Have the group sit around the table. Ask someone to sit on the edge of the table. Point out the impossibility of removing the napkin without tearing it. Then have the room lights extinguished.

Under cover of darkness, wet your fingers, then transfer the moisture to the napkin. This allows you to tear the napkin from the table leg silently. Fold the napkin and put it in your pocket. Then gently pull the duplicate napkin down from its hiding place.

Have the room lights turned on again. The napkin has jumped from one table leg to another.

If you can't get the room dark enough to perform the secret maneuvers under cover of total darkness, an alternative is to have those present close their eyes.

53   TELL THE TRUTH

This is a good trick to perform at a party in someone's home. Three spectators stand behind the magician. Two of the spectators hold dollar bills. The third holds a five-dollar bill. The third person raises his hand so that the others in the room know who has the five-dollar bill.

The magician remarks that the spectators are going to play a game similar to one on television. Each is to say, "I have the five-dollar bill." They should speak with sincerity. The magician will then try to determine which spectator is telling the truth.

The spectators each recite the line. Immediately the magician identifies the truthful spectator.

METHOD: The trick depends on the fact that it is performed in the living room because this is where the television set is most likely to be. Most people are not aware that the curved television screen is an excellent reflecting mirror. What the trick comes down to is that the magician arranges things so that he can glance into the television screen and see which spectator signals the audience that he has the five-dollar bill.

The rest is presentation. Pretend to study the way each spectator phrases his words when he says, "I have the five-dollar bill." Ask one or more spectators to repeat the words. Then reveal the truthful spectator.

54 SPOT REMOVER

In this trick a pencil or a letter opener is magically passed through a spectator's jacket without harming the jacket. As seen by the audience, the magician asks for the assistance of a spectator wearing a jacket. The jacket is removed and put on a coat hanger. This allows the spectator to hold up the coat by the hanger so all can see the trick.

Removing a piece of newspaper from his pocket, the magician says, "I saw an ad for a spot remover guaranteed to obliterate any spot on a man's jacket. It cost only a dollar. For my money I got this."

The magician removes a pencil from his pocket. "I was told to use the eraser end. Let's see if it works. We'll try it on your jacket."

The magician puts the pencil against the center of the spectator's jacket. Instantly the pencil completely penetrates the jacket without harming it.

METHOD: There are no gimmicks. Display the pencil as shown in Figure 212. Your other hand holds a large square of newspaper.

Note in Figure 212 that the newspaper is grasped between your left thumb and forefinger. Your other fingers are curled inward loosely. Note too that the newspaper is directly in front of the jacket sleeve. This is the key to the trick. Put the pencil behind the jacket. When it is out of sight, simply drop it down the jacket sleeve. It is secretly caught by your left fingers behind the newspaper.

Poke your right forefinger against the jacket, Figure 213. From the audience's view you appear to be poking the pencil against the

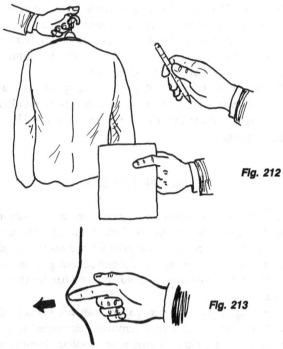

Fig. 212

Fig. 213

jacket. Say, "This looks like a good spot to remove." Bring the
newspaper up in front. The pencil is then grasped by your right
hand through the cloth, Figure 214. Some pencils have a knurled
metal cap at the eraser end. By rubbing your left thumbnail over
the metal cap, you can produce a noise that can be taken for a
ripping noise. The illusion produced by this noise is that the
pencil is ripping through the fabric.

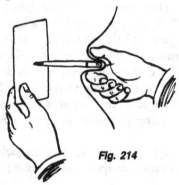

Fig. 214

Apologize to the spectator, saying, "I never thought it would work like this." Eventually push the pencil through the newspaper. Let it fall to the floor in front of the jacket. Say, "We've obliterated the spot. Frankly, I'm glad I tried this out on your jacket and not mine."

Take the newspaper out of the way to reveal that the jacket is unharmed.

You can use a letter opener or a butter knife instead of the pencil. Being heavier, these objects will slide down the sleeve faster. In a pinch you can even use a shot glass, a rubber ball or any small object that can be secretly dropped down the jacket sleeve.

Bob Read suggested a clever idea for tricks of this kind. With all attention on the pencil ripping through the jacket, it is an easy matter to pick the spectator's jacket pocket. As soon as your right hand is in back of the jacket, reach into the spectator's inside pocket and remove his wallet. Slip it into your own pocket. At a later time in the evening, you can do a bit of magical pickpocketing.

It is also easy to load an object into the spectator's inside jacket pocket. For example you can load a half dollar into his pocket. Later in the evening cause a half dollar to vanish by means of the Coin Fold (No. 14). The vanished coin is then made to reappear inside the spectator's jacket pocket.

CARDBOARD CONJURING

The best mind-reading tricks use simple props and straightforward handling to achieve their effects. The tricks in this chapter are done with apparatus made from cardboard or file-card stock. Such material is readily available at your local printer or business-supply house. You will find that printers have a large supply of file-card and cardboard stock in many sizes and colors. Since you want just the blank stock without any printing on it, you can obtain a generous supply at a nominal cost. The small investment is well worth it in terms of the effects that are produced.

55 TAILOR'S GHOST

The magician displays two blank pieces of shirt cardboard, explaining that they belonged to his late tailor, a man who knew everything about the shirt trade.

After being shown blank, the pieces of shirt cardboard are placed on the table in plain view. The magician asks the tailor's ghost to help out with an experiment. He has a man stand and announce his shirt size. The spectator might say that he has a 15″ collar and a 33″ sleeve.

The pieces of shirt cardboard are separated. Although they were blank a moment before, they now contain a message from the tailor's ghost. The message says: "15″ x 33″."

METHOD: Beforehand, you must learn the shirt size of a spectator in your audience. If you perform the trick for friends it is easy to get the required information from someone in the friend's family. Assuming his shirt size is 15″ by 33″, jot this down in chalk or marking pen on a blank piece of cardboard. Write the number 1 in the upper-left corner. Place this cardboard, writing-side up, under another piece of cardboard, Figure 215. Line up the two pieces so they are flush with one another. The blank cardboard is on top.

This is the only preparation. They key to the trick lies in the method of apparently showing both pieces of cardboard blank. For this purpose we will use a brilliant method of Jack Miller's.

With the blank cardboard on top, show the top surface and openly write the number 1 in the upper-left corner, Figure 216. Show the writing to the audience.

Turn both pieces of cardboard over end for end in the direction of the arrows shown in Figure 216. Write the number 2 in the upper left corner, Figure 217, then show this to the audience.

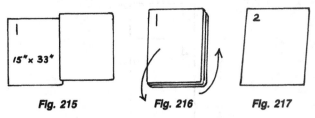

| Fig. 215 | Fig. 216 | Fig. 217 |

Slide the top cardboard to the right of the other cardboard, Figure 218, and place it underneath so that the number 2 shows. Then write the number 3 on the upper surface, Figure 219. Show the audience what you've written. Make sure the secret writing is not exposed to audience view.

Put the top cardboard under the other cardboard so that the 2 and 3 show, Figure 220. Again show the audience what you've written.

An important move comes into play at this point. Turn both pieces of cardboard end for end to the situation shown in Figure 221, but do so in such a way that only you can see the upper

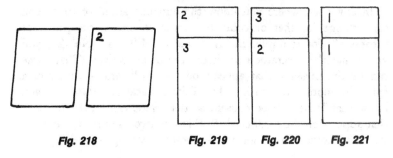

| Fig. 218 | Fig. 219 | Fig. 220 | Fig. 221 |

surfaces. This prevents the audience from seeing that each cardboard has a 1 on it.

We now use an idea of Burling Hull's. Convert the 1 on the uppermost cardboard to a 4. This is shown in Figure 222. Now show both sides of both pieces of cardboard to the audience, keeping them together, as in Figure 222. From the audience's point of view they have seen you number four blank surfaces. They have no reason to suspect that there is writing on one surface.

Square up the two pieces of cardboard. Lean them upright against a chair. Have the spectator stand and give his shirt size. Then separate the pieces of cardboard to show the mysterious writing.

Fig. 222

If you can't find out the spectator's shirt size, you can have the tailor's ghost reveal your own shirt size. The same trick can be done to produce more than one message. For example, follow the above procedure with two pieces of cardboard. Then follow the same procedure with two other pieces of cardboard. Show the tailor's first message, in which he reveals your shirt size. Then reveal the second message, which might be, "You should lose weight!" or some other comic message.

In any trick where you know the outcome ahead of time, you can arrange for that outcome to appear on one of the pieces of cardboard. For example, in "A Name in Millions" (No. 22) you know that the spectator will choose the name Wilson. That name can be the message that appears on the cardboard, courtesy of a spirit in another dimension. In "Take a Vacation" (No. 46) you know that Paris will be chosen, so that name can be the message that appears on the cardboard. In this way two completely different tricks are joined in a routine to produce a strong mystery.

56   A WINTER'S TALE

This is an excellent example of a trick in which the spectator reads the magician's mind. On the magician's table are five pictures. Clipped to each is a slip of paper containing the name of that picture. The titles are removed and placed face down in a glass.

The magician holds up the pictures so he alone can see them. He chooses one. The others are placed aside.

Now the spectator removes the slips of paper from the glass. There is a different title on each slip of paper. The spectator mixes them and chooses one. It might read, "December Eve."

The magician shows the pictures he did not choose. One shows a horse, another a car, another a building and the last a boat.

Then he turns around the picture he did choose. It is a winter landscape showing a farmhouse. The spectator picked the very title that matched the magician's picture.

There are no gimmicks. All of the titles are different. All of the paintings are different. The spectator chooses any title he likes, yet it matches the picture chosen by the magician.

METHOD: There is a subtle force at work here. Although all the titles are different, they describe the same picture.

At holiday time get a greeting card that shows a winter landscape. It might show a farmhouse with snow on the ground, a tree bare of leaves and a road leading to the farmhouse.

Pick up four other cards that do not relate in any way to the winter scene. Typically these might show a car, a building, a horse and a boat. Tourist postcards are a good source of such pictures. Mount each of the five pictures on its own square of cardboard. Once this preparation is done the apparatus will last many performances.

Also needed are five titles. They all describe the landscape, but in different ways. The titles might be "Evening in the Country," "The Old Farm," "December Eve," "Trees and Snow," "A Winter Night."

Fasten each title to the back of a painting with paper clips. When demonstrating the trick, show the paintings one at a time. Flip them over and show the title clipped to the back of each painting. Do this in a brief gesture so the audience can see the wording without having a chance to read it. The spectators should only be aware that all of the titles are different. This is reinforced by the fact that the words in each title are completely different from the others.

Remove all the title papers, turn them writing-side down and mix them. Then place them in a glass for the moment. Hold up the paintings so you alone can see them. Mix them about. Pretend to concentrate, then finally choose the landscape. Put the others aside picture-side down.

Tell the spectator to remove the title papers face down from the glass, mix them up and deal them out in a row face down on the table. He chooses any title.

When he's made a choice, take the remaining four titles and place them in your pocket. This gets rid of the evidence. Turn up each of the four paintings you didn't choose. Then have the spectator read aloud the chosen title. Finish by showing that the chosen painting exactly matched the spectator's title.

You can have four other pieces of paper in your pocket, each with a title that matches a painting. These can be brought out after the trick is over and left on the table to satisfy curious spectators.

Another way to present the trick is to use the food coupons that are carried by most newspapers. Choose, say, a dog-food coupon as the one you're going to pick later. The other four coupons should be obviously different. You might pick a soap-product, a baby-food, a pie-crust and a toothpaste coupon.

The titles are written on five different slips of paper. They might read, "Doggie Delight," "Pooch's Favorite," "Arf Biscuits," "Bow Wow" and one containing the actual name of the dog-food product. The rest of the handling is as described above.

57   MIND SCAN

The spectator is given two squares of cardboard like those shown in Figure 223. One has numbers written on it. The other has a triangle and a circle cut from it. While the magician goes into another room, the spectator puts the cardboard with the cutouts on top of the cardboard with the numbers so that two numbers show through the cutout windows, Figure 224.

The spectator announces the total of the two numbers. The

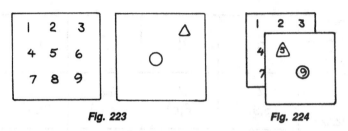

Fig. 223   **Fig. 224**

magician in the next room then reveals which two numbers were chosen. He then goes on to reveal which of the two numbers is the one inside the triangle!

METHOD: The numbers are written in the three-by-three array shown in Figure 223. Cut a triangle and a circle out of a matching square of cardboard. The triangle should be in the same position as the number 3, the circle in the same position as the number 5.

While you go into the next room, have the specator turn the cutout cardboard over end for end several times and turn it right to left at random so that the orientation of the cutouts could not possibly be known to you.

Then have him put the cardboard with the cutouts on top of the number square so that they are aligned. He then reads off the total of the two numbers that show in the windows, Figure 225. Remember this total.

Fig. 225

Tell him to slide the cutout cardboard either horizontally or vertically to some other position so that two other numbers show through the windows. He can't turn the cardboard over but he can slide it left or right, up or down. He might end up as shown in Figure 224. Tell him to announce the total of the two numbers.

This is all the information you need. Consulting the table shown in Figure 226, first find the entry in the top row for the first total, the one when the boards were aligned. In our example this total is 6, so you consult the first column of numbers on the left.

His second total was 14, as indicated in Figure 224. Consulting this entry in the first column you will find in parenthesis the

TOTAL WHEN BOARDS ARE ALIGNED	6	8	12	14
HIS TOTAL	14 (5,9)	14 (6,8)	14 (8,6)	14 (9,5)
	12 (4,8)	12 (5,7)	12 (7,5)	12 (4,8)
	8 (2,6)	8 (3,5)	8 (5,3)	8 (6,2)
	6 (1,5)	6 (2,4)	6 (4,2)	6 (5,1)

Fig. 226

numbers 5, 9. These are the two numbers he chose. The first will always be the number inside the triangle.

When constructing the cardboard with the cutouts, make sure the triangle and the circle are not too large. Also take care in filling out the cardboard with the numbers. The reason is that when the cardboard with the cutouts is placed on the number square, if it is aligned at an angle it should be impossible for the spectator to see numbers in both windows. In this way he is constrained to place the cardboard on top of the numbers in the correct manner.

58   V.I.P.

A subtle idea of Aage Darling's and a discovery made by George Kaplan are the ingredients in this mental mystery. Six spectators participate. Each jots down the name of a President of the United States. The magician's assistant then reveals each choice.

There are no codes. All of the articles can be borrowed.

METHOD: Needed is a square of cardboard measuring about 3" on a side. With the cardboard before you, rule off seven horizontal panels. Make the uppermost panel a little wider than the others, Figure 227.

Grasp the cardboard at the upper right corner, Figure 228, and turn it over to the position of Figure 229. As indicated by the X in the first three drawings, the upper right corner is now at the lower left. Rule six horizontal panels as shown in Figure 229.

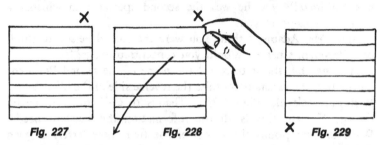

Fig. 227   **Fig. 228**   **Fig. 229**

Ask each of six spectators to whisper the name of a President to you. Jot them down in order from top to bottom in the six panels.

Turn the cardboard over by grasping it at the upper right corner and turning it down diagonally as in Figure 228. This brings the cardboard back to the position of Figure 227.

Ask each spectator in turn to whisper his last name to you. Jot down the names in order beginning with the second panel from the top. Leave the top panel blank. Then, using a pair of scissors, cut the cardboard into seven horizontal strips, Figure 230.

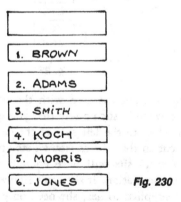

Fig. 230

You are holding all seven strips in your hand. The six with the spectator's names on them are dropped into a paper bag. The blank strip is kept in your hand. Immediately pick up a pad and pencil and place them in your hand, covering the slip. The blank slip is important because the back of it contains all the necessary information.

Your assistant is sitting with her back turned to the audience. Give her the pad and pencil. She also takes the blank strip.

Mix up the strips in the hat. Take out any strip and turn it so you can read the spectator's name. Say it is Adams. The number next to it tells you he was the second spectator to whisper a President's name to you.

Say, "Mr. Adams, I think you were the second person to think of a President's name. Would you concentrate on it?"

Hearing that she is to reveal the name of the second President on the list, the assistant consults the reverse side of the blank strip. It might look like Figure 231. Thanks to a discovery made by George Kaplan, this is all the information the assistant needs. With few exceptions the group of the first three letters of each President's name is unique and different from all the rest. In this case, knowing the first three letters are W-a-s, the assistant knows the chosen President must be Washington. She proceeds to reveal the name.

Continue in the same way with the other names. At the finish the assistant takes a bow.

NIX
WAS
LIN
EIS
KEN
JEF

Fig. 231

When you fill out the card with the names of the Presidents, make sure to write in such a way that you get the first three letters of the name close to the left side of the card. Even in cases where the card is cut so that the assistant gets only the first two letters, in most instances she will have enough information to proceed with a correct revelation. If she can't figure out the name from the information supplied to her, she need only say that she can't get a clear mental impression and will have to skip that name. This adds to the feeling of authenticity of the experiment since a real mind reader would have similar success.

59 JET THOUGHT

This brilliant trick, invented by J. G. Thompson, Jr., is so strong the audience is likely to suspect you use a confederate. For this reason be certain that the spectator you choose to assist is above suspicion.

The magician writes something on a card and puts it in an envelope. He explains that he wrote the name of a city on the card. He calls out the names of five cities he might stop at during an imaginary Boston-to-Dallas trip. The spectator is asked to guess which city the magician wrote on the card. The spectator might guess Denver. The magician opens the envelope, removes the card and shows he did indeed pick Denver.

METHOD: Needed are a stack of envelopes and five white file cards. The cards should be of a size to fit snugly into the envelope. A black crayon or marking pen is used to write on the cards.

The cards are going to be cut so they are graduated in size. On one card write "Denver" in large letters. On the second card write "St. Louis" and cut 3/16" off the long edge of this card. On the third card write "Chicago" and cut 3/8" from this card. On the fourth card write "New York" and cut 9/16" from this card.

Stack the cards, writing-side up, as follows: New York on top, then Chicago, St. Louis and Denver, in that order. Denver is the bottom card of the stack. Put the stack in one of the envelopes with the written sides toward the flap. When the cards are in place you will find that a step effect results, Figure 232. The step is clearly visible at the seam in the center of the envelope. Place this envelope on top of the stack of envelopes, Figure 233. Turn the stack over.

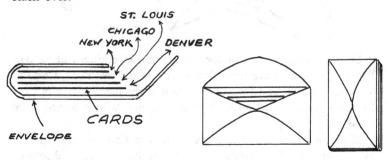

Fig. 232   **Fig. 233**

Place the fifth card in an empty envelope. Place this envelope on top of the stack and you are ready to perform. The envelope with the blank card is on top, the envelope with the other cards is on the bottom of the stack.

Say, "Usually I receive your thoughts. This time I want to send one of mine instead. In order for there to be no question later on, I'll jot down my thought on a card."

Remove the blank card from the top envelope. Then hand the envelope to the spectator for examination. When he's satisfied that it's ordinary, take it back and place it on top of the stack. Then hand him the blank card. When he looks at it, drop your hand to your side and turn over the stack of envelopes. This brings the prepared envelope to the top.

Place the blank card on top of the prepared envelope. Without showing the audience what you write, write "Dallas" in large letters on this card. To disguise the writing, you can write the last letter at the right, the next-to-last letter to the left of it, the next letter to the left of that and so on, so that the audience can't follow what you jot down on the card.

Remove the prepared envelope and put the rest of the envelopes aside. Insert this card into the envelope in back of the other cards. Make sure you hold the card and envelope vertically, Figure 234, so the audience can't see the writing. Put the envelope in a prominent place.

Fig. 234

Say to a volunteer spectator, "Imagine I'm taking a plane trip. We are going to leave from Boston and visit New York, Chicago, St. Louis, Dallas and Denver. I've writen the name of one of those five cities on the card sealed in that envelope. Which do you think it is?"

If necessary, repeat the names of the five cities slowly. As soon as the spectator has named a city, say to him, "You're absolutely right!"

Pick up the envelope, lift the flap and remove the correct card. This is a speedy operation, thanks to the previous preparation. Hand the card to the spectator and thank him for his cooperation.

The Dallas and Denver cards are the same size. It will be found that since they are the last cards on the stack, it is possible, with your thumb on the Denver card and your fingers on the Dallas card, to pull out either one with equal ease. With a bit of practice it is easy to find the proper card without looking. Hold the envelope with your left hand, open the flap with your right. As you talk to the audience, run the back of the fingernail of your right middle finger up along the cards. The fingernail will click off each card. Stop at the correct card and remove it from the envelope.

If you are willing to take a chance, say to the spectator, "Name any major city, like New York or Los Angeles." Chances are that he will name one of the cities in the envelope. Remove the appropriate card and it will appear that you correctly predicted which city the spectator would choose when asked to name any major city in the United States. This variation is the starting point for the following version of J. G. Thompson's routine.

60 THINK OF A PRESIDENT

The spectator is asked to think of a President of the United States. The magician holds up an envelope, saying that inside is a picture of a President. The spectator names the President he is thinking of. The envelope is opened and the picture removed. It is the President that the spectator named!

METHOD: Obtain photographs of Franklin Roosevelt, Eisenhower, Truman and Kennedy. Obtain drawings of Washington and Lincoln. Mount each on a piece of cardboard. Index the pieces of cardboard and arrange them in an envelope exactly as described in "Jet Thought" (No. 59). You are now ready to perform the routine.

Ask the spectator to name any President, explaining that you have a picture of the President already sealed inside the envelope. The spectator is most likely to name one of your six choices. When he names his choice, open the envelope and remove the appropriate picture.

There is an amusing way to get around the problem of the spectator naming an obscure President not covered by your choices. Put a baby's picture on the back of one of the pictures in the envelope. If the spectator names Harding, for example, open the envelope and remove the piece of cardboard with the baby's picture showing. Say, "This is of course Harding as a child." It gets a laugh. More important, the trick does not end in failure since the production of the baby's picture seems the intended point.

61   SOUP TO NUTS

"When magicians go out to a restaurant, they send a personal check ahead of time." The magician hands the spectator a sealed envelope. Inside is a check made out to the restaurant. The spectator is next given a menu. He chooses an appetizer, soup, entree and dessert. Each course is a different price. The bill might, for example, come to $21.00. The spectator removes the check from the envelope. Ths check is made out for exactly $21.00.

METHOD: This trick is based on a principle devised by Martin Gardner. Make up the menu cards shown in Figure 235. The appetizer card is printed on one side. The other cards have printing on both sides as shown. Place the four cards in your pocket until ready to perform.

Make out a personal check for $21, fold it and place it inside an envelope. Concealed inside the envelope is a folded dollar bill, Figure 236. Seal the envelope.

To present the trick, hand the sealed envelope to the spectator, explaining that this is your personal check that was sent ahead to pay for the meal.

Then remove the appetizer card from your pocket. Have the spectator choose either item. Say he picks the melon. Jot down the price of the melon on a piece of paper. Note the letter A next to melon. This tells you to show him the A side of the next card. In this case you would bring out the soup card with the chicken and beef side uppermost. Have him choose either chicken or beef soup. Say he picks beef. Jot down the price of beef soup on the piece of paper.

Note that beef soup has the letter B next to it. Remove the entree card with the B side (lasagna and stew) uppermost. Have

APPETIZER

A. MELON   3.00
B. ANTIPASTO   4.00

SOUP	A	SOUP	B
A. CHICKEN	2.00	A. TOMATO	1.00
B. BEEF	3.00	B. MUSHROOM	2.00

ENTREE	A	ENTREE	B
A. TURKEY	14.00	A. LASAGNA	13.00
B. STEAK	15.00	B. STEW	14.00

DESSERT	A	DESSERT	B
A. CAKE	2.00	A. ICE CREAM	1.00
B. PIE	3.00	B. NUTS	2.00

Fig. 235

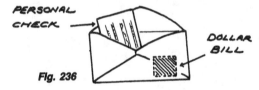

PERSONAL CHECK

DOLLAR BILL

Fig. 236

him make a choice. Say he picks lasagna. Jot down the price of
lasagna on the piece of paper.

Since lasagna has the letter A next to it, remove the dessert card
with the A side (cake and pie) showing. Say he picks cake. Jot
down the price of cake on the piece of paper. In our example the
bill would look like this:

Melon	$3.00
Beef soup	3.00
Lasagna	13.00
Cake	2.00
Total	$21.00

110 Self-Working Paper Magic

Tear open the end of the envelope. Have the spectator remove the personal check. He reads the amount and sees that you correctly predicted that the bill would total $21. Let the effect register, then shake out the dollar bill, saying, "And a dollar for the tip."

There is only one other outcome. In this case the bill will come to $22. A sample meal with this total is the following:

Antipasto	$4.00
Mushroom Soup	2.00
Lasagna	13.00
Pie	3.00
Total	$22.00

In this case have the spectator remove the check from the envelope and read it aloud. Your prediction is off by a dollar. Say, "My checking account was low so I could only write a check for $21. I settled the balance in cash." Now shake out the dollar bill from the envelope. It's an amusing and unexpected finish.

ROBERT E. NEALE'S PAPER MAGIC

Robert Neale's paper tricks are among the most clever and innovative in the field. Neale, a seminary professor and author, has combined paper folding and magic in strange new ways. This chapter is a sample of his fascinating inventions.

62 CONFETTI

Five seconds before midnight on New Year's Eve, the magician poured a glassful of confetti into an open paper tube. The confetti didn't fall out. Bewildered, the magician turned over the tube to look in the other end. The confetti still didn't pour out. When he turned the tube back, the confetti poured forth just in time to celebrate the new year.

METHOD: The tube is made from cardboard. The double construction is shown in Figure 237. It should be about 2½″ square and about 5″ long. The interior flaps are made from cardboard and are easily held in place with transparent tape. Decorate the top edge with colored decorator tape so top and bottom can be distinguished at a glance.

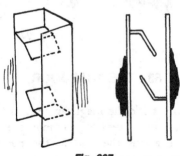

Fig. 237

Hold the tube as shown in Figure 238. Say that at midnight on New Year's Eve you poured confetti into a paper tube, intending to scatter it in the air. As you say this, pour confetti from a champagne glass into the top of the tube, Figure 239.

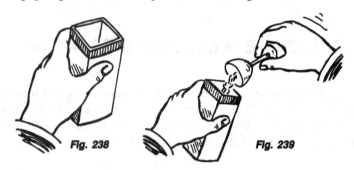

Fig. 238   Fig. 239

Act bewildered that the confetti didn't fall through. Turn your hand over, Figure 240, to check your watch. Say, "Then I realized I was five seconds too early." Note that the confetti still doesn't fall out.

When five seconds are up, turn the tube upright, but be sure to do it so the bottom of the tube is directly over a glass, Figure 241. The confetti will then fall out of the bottom of the tube into the glass. Say, "Right on time," and take your bow.

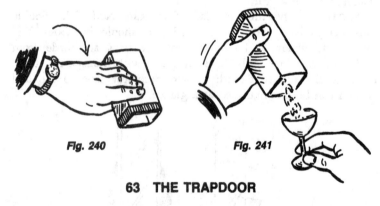

Fig. 240   Fig. 241

63 THE TRAPDOOR

In this astonishing trick the magician tears the center out of a playing card, saying he is creating an invisible trapdoor in the card. The spectator grasps the card at the point marked X in Figure 242. The playing card is *above* the spectator's hand.

The spectator closes his eyes or puts his hand behind his back. The magician makes a bit of magic. When the spectator opens his eyes, the playing card is *below* the spectator's hand, Figure 243!

The only way this surprising result could have occurred would be if the magician were somehow to have passed the playing card over the spectator's body.

Fig. 242   **Fig. 243**

METHOD: Cut the center from a playing card so that you are left with just the frame. Have the spectator grasp the card at point X as shown in Figure 244. If trying the trick for the first time, you can hold the card yourself between your thumb and forefinger.

Bend edge Y around as shown in Figure 245, so that it touches X as indicated in Figure 246. When the card is in this condition it can be held in position by your thumb and forefinger.

Then bend the sides around, Figure 247. The card will flip over to the position of Figure 248. It is now under your hand.

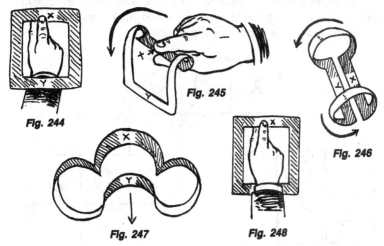

Fig. 244   **Fig. 245**   **Fig. 246**

Fig. 247   **Fig. 248**

Practice with a large piece of paper to get the knack of the handling. The end of the paper marked X in Figure 244 can be clamped under a heavy book to keep it in place. Both hands will then be free to do the manipulation. With a few minutes' practice you will be able to perform the handling very quickly.

This trick makes a good encore to "Reaching through a Playing Card" (No. 29). If a spectator tells you that he knows that trick, switch to Neale's "The Trapdoor" and you will fool the spectator.

64   TV PUZZLE

This puzzle consists of a folded piece of paper that looks like Figure 249. There is a face in one panel. Circular TV screens have been cut in two other panels. The back of the puzzle has one more TV screen. The task is to fold the paper in such a way as to get the smiling face behind one of the screens. The puzzle can be folded in any direction as long as no new creases are made.

This puzzle is an excellent example of how people will make self-limiting assumptions that prevent them from finding the solution to a problem. In the present case most people assume the solution will be brought about by folding the paper from one flat pattern to another. In fact the puzzle can only be solved by converting it to a three-dimensional box.

The paper consists of nine unit squares. Cut out three circular screens, draw tuning knobs and a face, and lightly mark an A and an X, all exactly as shown in Figure 250.

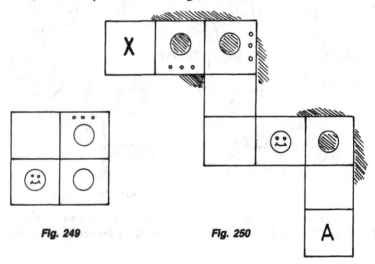

Fig. 249   Fig. 250

Turn the paper over side for side (left to right). Draw tuning knobs and lightly mark a B and a Y, as shown in Figure 251. The letters A, B, X, Y are only for the purpose of learning the method of construction. Once you know how to make the folds, don't letter the panels.

Bring the paper back to the position shown in Figure 250. Fold the dotted panels of Figure 252 underneath and to the right. Then fold the dotted panels of Figure 253 up in back. Fold the dotted panels of Figure 254 underneath and down.

The panel shown as an upside-down Y in Figure 254 rests on top of a TV screen. Move this panel to a position under the screen, bringing you to the position of Figure 255.

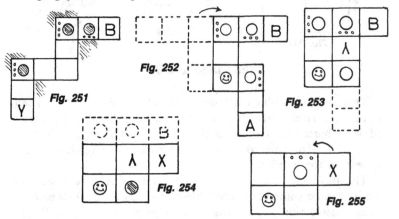

Fig. 251   Fig. 252   Fig. 253   Fig. 254   Fig. 255

Fold panel X in back, in the direction of the arrow in Figure 255. This will bring panels A and B together. Fasten them together with glue or tape. This completes the construction.

To solve the puzzle, hold it as shown in Figure 249 with the smiling face in the lower left panel. Fold the left edge over onto the right, Figure 256. You now have a double-thickness rectangle. Fold the left edge of the upper layer of the rectangle to the right, forming the square of Figure 257.

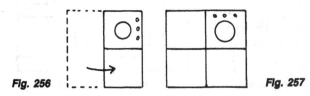

Fig. 256   Fig. 257

Fold the upper half of the square, shown dotted in Figure 258, down in back. The square has become a rectangle again. This rectangle is going to become a three-dimensional TV set. Push the left side and the right side together. The box will open as shown in Figure 259. To open out the box you may have to use your fingers to separate the folds. The panel containing the smiling face and the front panel containing the TV screen are each of a single thickness.

You've created a TV set. Peer through the screen to see the face.

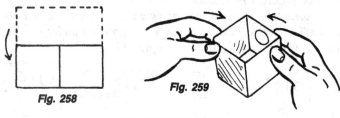

Fig. 258   **Fig. 259**

65   INSIDE OUT

This is a tube which has the remarkable ability to turn itself inside out. To distinguish inside from outside, the tube is decorated with horizontal stripes on the outside and vertical stripes on the inside. The tube is flexed and instantly the vertical stripes appear on the outside.

The inside-out tube can be made from paper, but a sturdier model can be constructed from file-card or postcard stock or even from construction paper. The starting point is shown in Figure 260. The length from A to B is about 2″. BD, DE and EF are each 2″ in length. Crease both ways along the dotted lines so that the paper will fold easily.

By adding vertical and horizontal stripes it can be made to perform the trick of apparently turning itself inside out. Figure 261 shows the stripes added to the front. Turn the paper over side for side. Then draw the stripes shown in Figure 262.

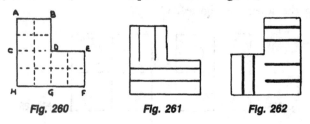

Fig. 260   **Fig. 261**   **Fig. 262**

To construct the inside-out tube, turn it back to the position of Figure 260. Fold DEFG over to the left, Figure 263, and fasten it to CH with tape. Fold ABCD back and down so that AB meets GH, Figure 264. Tape AB to GH. This completes the construction.

Push the sides, Figure 265. The paper will open out into the tube shown in Figure 266. The horizontal stripes are on the inside of the tube. The vertical stripes are on the outside.

Flatten the tube, then push in from the top and bottom, in the direction of the arrows in Figure 267. The tube will now open the other way. Stand it upright. As shown in Figure 268, the vertical stripes are now on the inside.

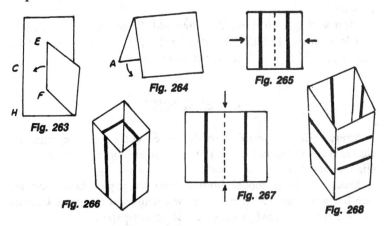

Fig. 263   Fig. 264   Fig. 265   Fig. 266   Fig. 267   Fig. 268

66 STRIPES MAKE YOU THINNER

This is a trick using the inside-out tube. As seen by the audience, the magician places a box on the table. From it he removes a tube with vertical stripes and one with horizontal stripes. He asks the audience, "Which tube looks thinner?"

The answer is that the tube with vertical stripes looks thinner. The magician removes this tube from the box. He then says, "It's well known that horizontal stripes make you look fatter." He pauses, then adds, "But not this fat." The box is tipped over. The other tube has changed into a large striped rubber ball!

METHOD: Besides the inside-out tube you will need a large white rubber ball. Paint stripes around it. Put the inside-out tube and the rubber ball into a plain cardboard box. The inside-out tube is arranged so the outer stripes are horizontal.

Say, "I've been told that vertical stripes make you thinner. Let's see if you agree."

Reach into the box and bring out the inside-out tube with both hands. Stand it on end on the table. Mention that it's decorated with horizontal stripes. Say, "Which do you think looks taller—this one or this one?"

Pick up the tube with both hands and lower it back into the box. As soon as it's out of sight, fold it so it opens the other way. Bring it out and place it on the table so that it looks like a vertically striped tube. Say, "This tube has the same dimensions as the other, but the stripes are vertical. Do you think it looks thinner?"

Most will agree it does. You then add, "Horizontal stripes make you look fatter, but this is ridiculous!" Tip the box over and let the large rubber ball bounce out onto the table.

67   STRETCHIT

Stretchit is a companion to the inside-out tube. The construction is similar, but rather than turning inside out, the stretchit tube changes its shape.

Make the basic model from a piece of paper. Once you are familiar with the construction and working, you can make sturdier models from file-card stock or construction paper.

Referring to Figure 269, AH is 4". AB is 1"; AC and HF are 2". Crease the paper along the dotted lines so that it will fold easily. You can fold first one way, then the opposite way to make it easier to handle the model later.

Construction is as follows. Fold DEFG over so EF lines up with CH, Figure 270. Fasten EF to CH with tape.

Fold ABCD down in back of the paper so that AB lines up with GH, Figure 271. Fasten AB to GH with tape. This completes the construction.

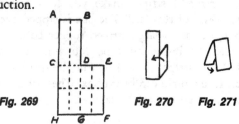

Fig. 269   *Fig. 270*   *Fig. 271*

Holding the tube flat in your hand, apply slight pressure to the sides as indicated by the arrows in Figure 272. The tube will instantly spring open to form a long rectangular tube.

Flatten the tube. Then apply pressure to the ends as shown by the arrows in Figure 273. The tube will spring open again, but now it forms a perfectly square tube as shown in Figure 274.

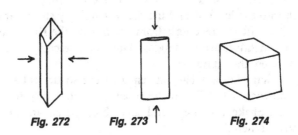

Fig. 272   **Fig. 273**   **Fig. 274**

68 FLEXIBLE TRANSPO

Two tubes are constructed like the stretchit tube. They exchange places in bewildering fashion. The trick has a surprise ending.

Two stretchit tubes are required. One is folded to look like a square and one like a rectangle. Also needed is a bottle of soda that just fits inside the rectangular tube. Small plastic replicas of soda bottles are easily obtained in toy stores. Two plain cardboard boxes are needed. They should be large enough to conceal the apparatus from audience view when the apparatus is lowered into the cardboard box.

Show two empty boxes. Then show the rectangular tube and place it in one box. Place the square tube in the other box. As soon as the square is out of sight, fold it so the shape changes into the rectangle.

Ask, "Where's the rectangle?" The audience just saw you put the rectangle in the box on the left. They will point to the left box. Start to reach into that container, act surprised, as if the transposition just took place before your eyes, then reach into the container on the right and show the rectangle.

Replace the rectangle in the box on the right. Immediately fold it so the shape changes back into the square. Ask, "We might have better luck with the square. Where is it?" Since you just placed the rectangle in the box on the right, the audience will assume the square is on the left.

Start to reach into the container on the left, act surprised, then reach into the box on the right and remove the square.

For the finish, replace the square in its container, but immediately fold it so it changes back to a rectangle. Say, "The only way this trick could work is if there's two of everything."

Reach into the left box and lift the rectangle by sliding it off the bottle. Then lift the rectangle from the box on the right, showing that you had duplicate rectangles. Drop both rectangles into the empty box on the right.

Say, "I don't know what happened to the square tubes."

The audience will tell you the squares are obviously in the box on the left. Shake your head and say, "No, the square isn't here. The bottle is here."

Tip over the box and allow the bottle of soda to roll out for the surprise finish.

Note that in the trick the rectangular tube need not be prepared since it is just a tube and is not manipulated like the stretchit tube in the other box. If you can't find a bottle of soda to fit, you can use dice or a box of cookies instead.

69   STRETCH A BILL

This is a subtle variation of the stretchit tube. It is made from a dollar bill. Although you construct the apparatus in front of the spectators, when they try it with their own dollar bills, they will find it impossible to make a shape-changing tube.

To prepare, fold a dollar bill in quarters, Figure 275. Fold over the endmost quarters to arrive at the shape shown in Figure 276. Then crease the bill as shown by the dotted lines in Figure 276 to form four squares. There will be about an inch left over at the right end. Each square is about 1 5/16" on a side. The secret preparation which makes the trick work is done here. Slit the bill along the second crease from the left as indicated in Figure 276.

Fold the bill into a square tube as shown in Figure 277. The tube will change shape according to the method already described. Apply pressure to the sides or to the ends and the tube will change from a rectangle into a square.

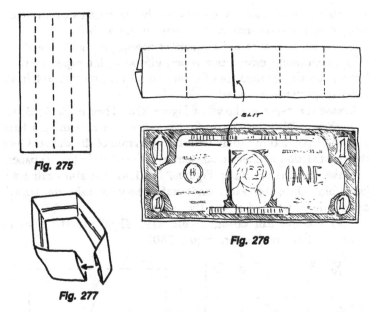

Fig. 275

Fig. 276

Fig. 277

The best way to present the trick is to prepare the bill as described above. Then open the bill so it is flat. Keep it in your wallet until you are ready to perform. When you do the trick, fold it as indicated in Figure 276, then tuck the end in as shown in Figure 277. The slit in the bill does not show and if you are careful with the handling the slit will not open up during the construction of the stretchit tube.

Display the square tube. Then press it flat, apply pressure and it will open into a rectangle. Spectators who saw you construct the tube will think they can duplicate the feat. Not knowing about the slit in the bill, they are guaranteed to fail. After demonstrating the trick, put away the apparatus. When someone asks to see it, remove a duplicate from your pocket. The duplicate is a square tube made from a dollar bill but it has no slit. After examining this bill the audience will still be in the dark as to how it's done.

70 NEALE'S SHORTCHANGE WALLET

Bob Neale's shortchange wallet allows you to switch objects in an undetectable manner. Remarkably, the wallet can be made from a single square of paper. We will describe the wallet's construction first, then a shortchange routine you can do with it.

To make the wallet use a square of newspaper measuring about 12" on each side. Construction paper, gift-wrapping paper, cloth or leather can also be used, but for the shortchange routine to follow, a newspaper wallet is ideal.

Crease the paper as shown in Figure 278. Then mark A, B, C, D as shown. These marks are for the purpose of explaining a later fold and have nothing to do with the operation of the wallet. Once the construction is understood there is no need to letter the paper.

Make the cuts shown in Figure 278. This will also facilitate a later fold. Once the reader understands how to make the wallet, there will be no need to cut the paper.

Fold the top half down, Figure 279. Then fold the sides in about ¼" from the center, Figure 280.

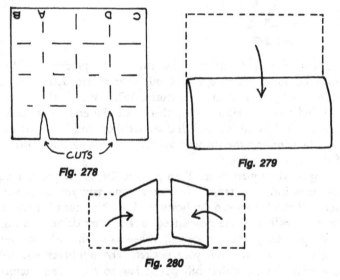

Fig. 278

Fig. 279

Fig. 280

Construction is almost complete. With the apparatus in front of you, it will look like Figure 281. A, B, C, D are just inside the front flaps. Lift up the front flaps. A, B, C, D are then folded up inside the wallet as shown by the arrows in Figure 282. The first part of this action, in which A–B is folded up on the left side, is indicated in Figure 283. After A–B and C–D have been tucked up into place the wallet will look like Figure 284.

Tuck E up inside the wallet. Then tuck F up inside the wallet. You are now at the position indicated in Figure 285. Finish by tucking G up inside the wallet.

This completes the construction. The wallet has two compartments for bills as shown by the arrows in Figure 286. It is this feature which allows you to switch objects with the shortchange wallet.

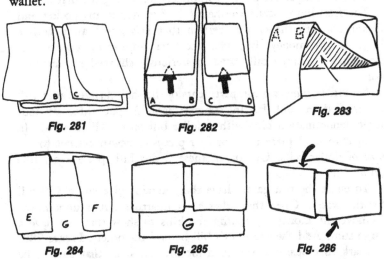

Fig. 281   Fig. 282   Fig. 283

Fig. 284   Fig. 285   Fig. 286

Experienced paper folders will have no trouble constructing the wallet without cutting the paper. Smaller wallets can be made for tricks using postage stamps, coins or other small objects. A sample shortchange routine is described next.

71 THE CON ARTIST

This is a demonstration of how the shortchange artist works. By showing your audience what to look for, you will help them avoid getting swindled by a skillful con man. In this classic confidence game the con artist sets up shop on a busy street corner. He is selling attractive designer watches for $20 each. The prospective buyer picks out a style he likes and gives the con man $20. The con man puts the money in his wallet. As he does, he flashes the other bills in the wallet, showing that he has a large sum.

The con man looks in a cardboard box that contains his

inventory but can't find the style the buyer wants. He apologizes, saying that his partner took all the expensive watches, leaving him with the cheap ones.

He appears confused by this unexpected turn of events and says, "Here's your money back." Reaching into the wallet, he takes out *all* the cash and hands it over. Still confused, he turns his attention to another prospective buyer, completely forgetting the first buyer.

The first buyer stuffs the handful of money in his pocket and disappears into the crowd, certain that he's going away with a huge sum of money. But when he later empties his pockets, he finds that the large bills have mysteriously changed to worthless paper.

METHOD: The two compartments of the shortchange wallet will be labeled A and B. In compartment A put three or four large-denomination bills with a dollar bill on top, Figure 287. In compartment B place three or four pieces of newspaper cut to the size of dollar bills. On top of these bogus bills place a genuine dollar bill.

To enact the con game, have the spectator give you a $20 bill for the watch. Open the wallet so compartment A is uppermost. Remove the money, spreading the bills to show that you have a large sum. Add the spectator's bill behind the others, Figure 288. Remark that business was good for the con artist that day, so he had a lot of money.

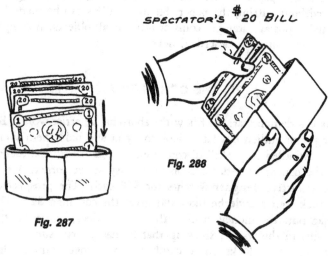

SPECTATOR'S $20 BILL

Fig. 288

Fig. 287

Return the bills to the wallet, Figure 289. With your left hand flip the top of the wallet over so the wallet is closed. Hold it in your right hand, Figure 290.

Remark that at this point the con artist would rummage through a box of inventory and discover he didn't have the watch the buyer wanted. The con artist then offers to refund the money. As this is said, flip the wallet over onto your left palm, Figure 291, and let it spring open, Figure 292. Reach into compartment B and remove the contents. Fold it so the dollar bill is on the outside and the plain paper on the inside. Hand it to the spectator. The spectator stuffs it into his pocket, realizing only later that he was swindled.

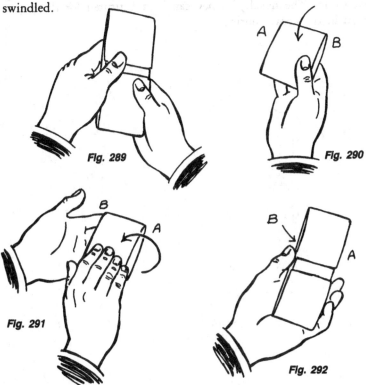

Fig. 289

Fig. 290

Fig. 291

Fig. 292

Bob Neale suggests that you acquire a foreign-language newspaper if possible. Make up the wallet from that paper. A Chinese newspaper will suggest certain patter stories, a Spanish paper other stories, and so on.

Note too that the wallet can be gimmicked like the "Improved Buddha Papers" (No. 50), with a slit in the bill compartment. This would allow you to feed a small object from one compartment to the other. Thus you tell the buyer to give you half the money in cash, the other half by check. Fold the check and feed it through compartment A into compartment B. Then take the spectator's cash and put it in compartment A. After you make the switch, hand the spectator the worthless bills plus his own check. Seeing that he is getting back the check he just gave you, he will never suspect a switch.

Novelty stores sell play money which, at a glance, looks like the real thing. The novelty money can be substituted for the paper strips in the above routine.

FURTHER PAPER MAGIC

This chapter contains tricks that have strong visual impact. In one, a star mysteriously materializes before the spectator's eyes. In another, a hole punched in one piece of paper migrates to another piece of paper. In yet another trick, the spectator's first and last names, written by the spectator on a piece of paper, instantly change places.

72 THE MYSTIC STAR

In this amazing trick two cards are shown to be blank on both sides. When they are held up to the light, Figure 293, a star gradually materializes on one card. Just the two cards are used.

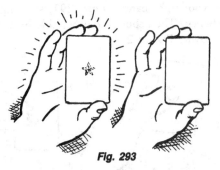

Fig. 293

METHOD: This trick, originally published by Will Goldston, makes uses of a fake turnover that has many applications. It is used here to conceal the presence of a star on one of the cards. The cards should be of thin cardboard. Blank business cards or blank postcards are ideal. The cards should be about the size of playing cards.

In the center of one card draw a star. The star should be of a size that can be covered by your thumb and therefore concealed from audience view. When drawing the star don't bear down too hard because you don't want an impression of the star to show through on the other side of the card.

At the start of the routine have the blank card in your left hand, the star card in your right hand. Your right thumb covers the star, Figure 294. Display the star card on both sides, taking care not to let the audience see the star by keeping the thumb firmly in place. Then drop this card star-side down into your left hand, Figure 295, on top of the blank card.

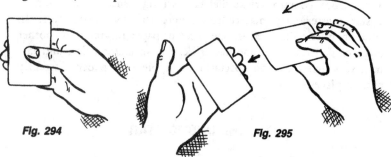

Fig. 294   Fig. 295

Turn over both cards as a unit by curling your fingers in, Figure 296. Then flip both cards over again. The star card will be on top. Push the blank card out from under the star card with your left fingers. Take it in your right hand, Figure 297, showing the blank surface to the audience. Then show the other side by turning your right hand palm down, Figure 298.

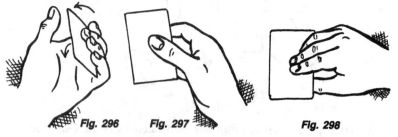

Fig. 296   Fig. 297   Fig. 298

The fake turnover comes into play at this point. With the aid of this deceptive move you will apparently show both sides of the star card to be blank. Curl your left thumb under the star card, Figure 299. As your left hand turns over to a palm-down position, the star card is levered up almost to a vertical position, Figure 300.

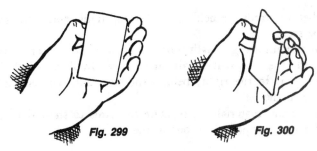

Fig. 299   Fig. 300

Note that the card is gripped between your left thumb and forefinger. To complete the move, turn your left hand palm down, Figure 301.

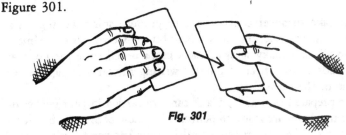

Fig. 301

To provide some slight but necessary misdirection for the move, your right hand begins to turn palm up just a fraction of a second before your left hand begins to turn palm down. The eye tends to follow the moving object, so audience attention will focus first on your right hand.

In Figure 301 your left hand is palm down and your right hand is palm up. Apparently both sides of both cards have been shown. Toss the star card onto the blank card in your right hand, in the direction of the arrow in Figure 301.

Grasp both cards between your right middle finger and thumb, Figure 302. Note that the cards are separated. Because of this separa-

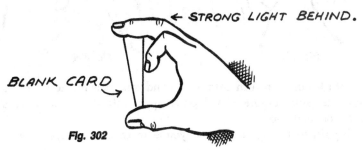

← STRONG LIGHT BEHIND.

BLANK CARD →

Fig. 302

tion, when the cards are held up to a strong light source, the star won't be seen.

If your forefinger gradually pushes the star card closer to the blank card, the star will slowly materialize. In Figure 302 the light source is to the right, behind the star card. The audience should be to the left.

After the star materializes, separate the cards to show that the star has actually appeared on one of the cards.

73 ALMOST CERTAINLY

The fake turnover can be used to produce spirit writing on a blank card. For example, on a blank business card write, "Almost certainly!" in a shaky scrawl. Use a green pencil since the unusual color adds to the effect of ghostly writing mysteriously appearing on one of the cards.

The prepared card and a blank card are carried in your pocket or wallet until you are ready to perform. To show both cards blank on both sides, take the prepared card in your left hand, writing-side down. Take the blank card in your right hand. Hold them on your palms. As you are about to turn over both cards, curl your left thumb under the prepared card, Figure 303.

As your hands are turned palm down, push your left thumb against its card to lever it upright. At the same time curl your left forefinger against the bottom of the card, Figure 304.

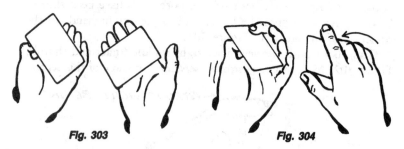

Fig. 303   Fig. 304

Both hands then turn palm down and toss their respective cards onto the table, Figure 305. You've apparently shown both cards blank on both sides.

Explain to the spectator that you're in touch with spirits who

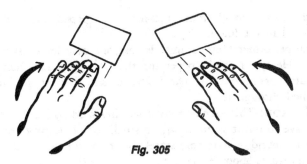

Fig. 305

can see the future. Have the spectator ask a question about a future event. He might ask, "Will I win the lottery?"

Place the two cards together, writing on the inside. Make mystic passes over the cards, mumble a few mysterious words, then separate the cards to show the answer to the spectator's question.

To take into account the opposite outcome, write "Almost certainly!" on one card, "Almost certainly not!" on another. When you display the cards in Figure 303, each is writing-side down. Perform the fake turnover with both cards as you apparently turn them over and toss them onto the table.

Ask the spectator about a future event he wants answered. He might ask, "Will I get fired?" This time you would choose the "Almost certainly not!" card as the proper answer to his question.

The spectator might not frame his question for a yes or no answer. For example, he might ask, "Should I buy the golf clubs or the fishing rod?" In this case restate his question so it can logically be answered by yes or no. In the example, you might say, "John wants to know if he should buy the golf clubs." Now display either card as the spirit's answer to his question.

Since the side with the writing is never seen until the end, you can make the writing in large, bold letters with a marking pen.

74 ENDPAPERS

The performer removes two pieces of paper from a pad. One sheet is taken by the spectator. The performer keeps the other piece of paper. Each person folds his paper into quarters.

A ticket punch or paper punch is then used to punch a hole through the magician's folded piece of paper. Since the paper punch goes through four thicknesses of paper, four holes are produced in the folded sheet.

The performer then commands that one hole leave his piece of paper. He opens up the paper and there are only three holes. The spectator opens out his paper and is surprised to find a hole punched through it.

METHOD: This excellent trick was invented by Lu Brent. First you have to outfit yourself with a small, one-hole paper punch of the kind found in stationery stores. Next you'll need a pad of paper that measures about 3″ square.

Punch a hole in one corner of the third sheet down from the top of the pad, Figure 306. This is the extent of the preparation.

To perform, tear off the top sheet of the pad, fold it in quarters and punch a hole through the four thicknesses. The patter is that you want to see if the punch is working properly, but actually it conditions the spectator to expect that when the next sheet is punched, it too will have four holes.

Now the next two sheets are torn off together. Hold them slightly fanned in your hand, Figure 307. Your thumb and forefinger conceal the hole in the prepared sheet.

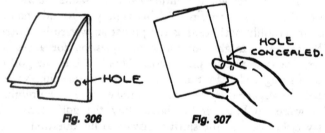

Fig. 306   Fig. 307

Square up the two sheets. The prepared sheet is under the other sheet. Fold them in half by bringing the top half toward you, Figure 308. Then pull out the inner sheet, Figure 309, and give it to the spectator. Fold your sheet in quarters by bringing the left half over in back of the right half, Figure 310. This puts the hole inside the folded paper. Have the spectator follow along with his paper, so that the unprepared sheet is also folded in quarters.

Now exchange sheets with the spectator. Pick up the paper punch and apparently punch through the four thicknesses of paper. Actually the jaws of the paper punch engage only the top three thicknesses, Figure 311.

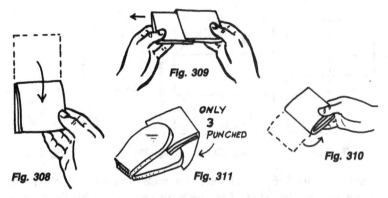

Fig. 309

ONLY
3
PUNCHED

Fig. 310

Fig. 308

Fig. 311

Say the magic word, then open your paper. You can delay the climax by putting thumb and forefinger on the part of the paper where the supposed fourth hole would be. With a rubbing motion you apparently cause the hole to close up. Remove your hand and the hole has vanished.

The spectator opens his paper and is surprised to discover that the hole has transported itself to his paper.

75 SHARPSHOOTER

This is a dramatic way to reveal the name of a chosen card. The magician forms a popgun out of a sheet of blank paper. When the gun is given a sharp downward motion it opens with a bang. The name of a previously chosen card is seen to have somehow appeared on the paper.

METHOD: Two things need to be explained—the method of making the paper gun and the method of forcing a card which will later appear on the paper.

To construct the gun, a sheet of 8½"x11" writing paper is first folded in half vertically and horizontally. Open out the paper. Print the name of the force card, in the abbreviated form, shown in Figure 312. We'll assume the force card is the ♣A.

Turn the paper over end for end to bring the blank side up. This completes the preparation. To present the trick have the paper on the table so the blank side shows. Fold the corners in as indicated in Figure 313. Then fold the right side over, Figure 314. Fold A up to the center as shown in Figure 315. Then fold B down to the

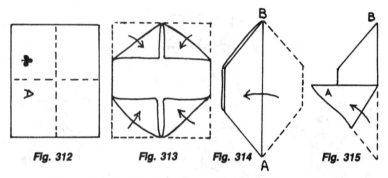

Fig. 312   Fig. 313   Fig. 314   Fig. 315

center, Figure 316. All of the above folds are done with the paper lying flat on the table. The spectator sees only a blank sheet of paper and is unaware of the secret writing.

The upper triangle is now folded down in back, bringing you to the position of Figure 317. This completes the formation of the popgun. At no time does the secret writing show.

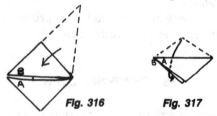

Fig. 316   Fig. 317

To force the ♣A we will use a method devised by Ed Balducci. Beforehand, arrange to have the ♣A on top of the deck. Hand the deck to the spectator. Tell him to lift a packet from the top of the deck, turn it face up and place it back on top. Then have him lift a larger packet from the top, turn it over and place it back on top. There will be several face-up cards on top of the pack at this point. Have him spread the cards and note the first face-down card. This will be the ♣A.

Form the popgun, following the instructions that bring you to Figure 317. Then turn the popgun over, Figure 318. Grasp it at AB between your right thumb and forefinger. Give the popgun a sharp downward snap and it will open with a bang, Figure 319, to reveal the name of the chosen card. Patter is to the effect that a sharpshooter friend once taught you how to take aim at the deck and fire a round at the chosen card. Snap the popgun to produce the name of the chosen card. If you go through the slight added

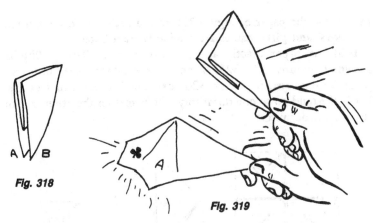

Fig. 318

Fig. 319

preparation of having a duplicate ♣A in the deck with a small hole in it, you can then spread the deck to show that you fired a bullet right through the chosen card.

For more information on card-forcing methods, see the chapter on the subject in *More Self-Working Card Tricks* (Dover 24580-2).

76   THE BOYS FROM THE GIRLS

The paper fold used to make the popgun in "Sharpshooter" (No. 75) has an offbeat application to an entirely different trick. On a square piece of paper lightly mark off 16 squares. Place the names of girls in each of the center squares and also in the corner square, Figure 320. Fill in the other squares with the names of boys. The paper appears to be a random listing of boys' and girls' names.

EVA	BILL	BOB	MARY
JOE	LIZA	ALICE	TOM
JACK	JILL	EVE	ADAM
BETH	SAM	TIM	ANN

Fig. 320

The patter story is to the effect that, at a certain coed summer camp, it was necessary to reserve rooms for 16 campers in two dormitories. The kids filled in their names on a sheet of paper like this. Show the paper of Figure 320 to the audience. Let them see that boys' and girls' names are randomly distributed.

Fold the paper exactly as in "Sharpshooter." The folding is shown in Figures 321–325. Then cut the folded paper into two pieces as indicated in Figure 326. Explain that the names on the left half would go to one dormitory, the names on the other half to the second dormitory.

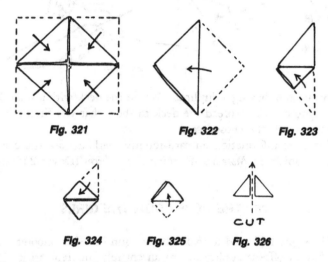

Fig. 321   **Fig. 322**   **Fig. 323**

Fig. 324   **Fig. 325**   **Fig. 326**

The kids expected coed dormitories, but when the left packet was opened, it contained only boys' names. When the right packet was opened, it contained only girls' names.

To add an atmosphere of mystery you can borrow from an idea described in "Paradox Papers" (No. 9). Hand someone a packet of eight playing cards and have him pick one. Write down the name of this card in a square where a girl's name would appear in the previous description. Then write down the names of the other seven cards in squares where boys' names would appear.

Have another spectator name any geometric symbol. Draw it in a blank square where a boy's name would appear. Then draw seven other symbols in the remaining blank squares. Fold up the paper and cut it as described above. When the two groups are examined it will be found that the chosen card appears in the group of squares with the symbols, and the chosen symbol appears in the group of squares with the playing cards.

77 CORRECTING FLUID

In this amusing trick the wrong prediction instantly changes to the correct prediction. The apparatus is made from a piece of stiff paper measuring about 3″ in width and 9″ in length. Fold it across the middle as shown in Figure 327. Then bring the top half down so it is even with the bottom half, Figure 328.

Cut slots AB through both thicknesses of paper as shown in Figure 328. Open out the paper, Figure 329. Cut from C to D to form the two flaps X and Y shown in Figure 329. Put the scissors aside as they will no longer be needed.

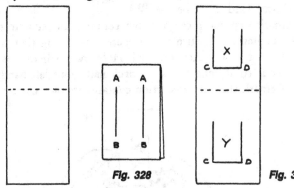

Fig. 327   Fig. 328   Fig. 329

Fold the paper in half across the middle. Then draw the back flap up in front of the front flap, Figure 330.

On the uppermost flap write ♥8 as shown in Figure 331. Bear down with the pen so that an impression is transferred through the paper.

Open out the paper. On the blank flap write ♥3 as shown in Figure 332. Trace over the impression so that ♥3 is in exactly the same position on this flap as ♥8 is on the other.

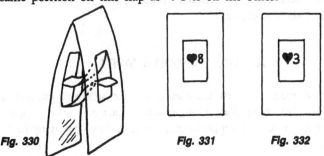

Fig. 330   Fig. 331   Fig. 332

Now draw the ♥8 flap up in front of the ♥3 flap. The apparatus will look like Figure 331 at this point. This completes the preparation. Place the prepared paper on the table, writing side down.

It is necessary to force the ♥3 on the spectator. An easy way to do this is to use the Balducci force described in "Sharpshooter" (No. 75). In this case have the ♥3 on top of the pack. Have the spectator turn over a small group of cards on top so they are face up. He then grasps a larger packet and turns it over on top. He spreads the top face-up cards until he comes to the first face-down card. This will be his card. If the above handling has been followed correctly, the chosen card must be the ♥3.

Remark that the piece of paper contains an accurate prediction of the chosen card. Turn up the paper, revealing that the prediction shows the ♥8. Act confused. Hold the prediction as in Figure 333. Your right hand holds the back half, your left hand the front half. Remark that the prediction contains its own correcting fluid.

Fig. 333

With your left hand raise the top layer with a short, quick movement. The result is that the ♥8 flap will be pulled away, revealing the ♥3 flap. The movement is too fast to be detected by the eye. The result from the spectator's point of view is that with a flick of the wrist you caused the ♥8 to change to the ♥3. The illusion is that part of the 8 erased itself to produce the 3. The prediction now shows the correct card.

78 THE CAPTAIN'S SHIRT

There are many versions of a classic trick in which newspaper is folded and torn to produce a succession of hats and other shapes. This version, by Lillian Oppenheimer, is considered by many to be the best.

The story is told of a boy who didn't know what he wanted to be when he grew up. He thought about a variety of roles, from fireman to Robin Hood. As the boy's story is related to the audience, it is illustrated with a newspaper which is folded into a variety of hats. The newspaper turns into a boat and then into a shirt for the surprise finish. The shirt is large enough for a child to wear.

The remarkable feature of this routine is that you require only a sheet of newspaper to perform it. There are no other props. The folds are simple to make, yet they illustrate the story in a vivid and amusing manner. The appearance of the shirt at the finish comes as a complete surprise.

METHOD: You can use a tabloid-size sheet measuring about 15″ by 22″ or a full-size sheet which measures about 22″ by 28″. The larger-size sheet is preferred because it produces a shirt large enough to be worn by a child.

Open the sheet to its full length. Fold it in half each way and open it out flat again, Figure 334. If you are performing this routine for the first time it will be easier to label A, B, C, D as shown so you can refer to these corners during the course of the handling.

You tell the story of a boy who lived by the sea. He didn't know what he wanted to be when he grew up, so he took a walk one day to think things out. As you say this, fold the top half of the paper down so it is even with the bottom half, Figure 335.

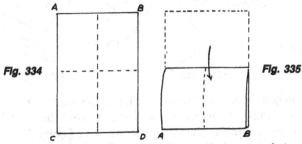

Fig. 334   **Fig. 335**

Fold the upper left and upper right panels in toward the center, Figure 336. Fold up AB in front, Figure 337. Then fold CD up in back to the position shown in Figure 338. Fold down A and B in front, Figure 339A. Then fold down C and D in back, Figure 339B. Put on the hat, Figure 340, as you say, "He thought he might want to be a captain."

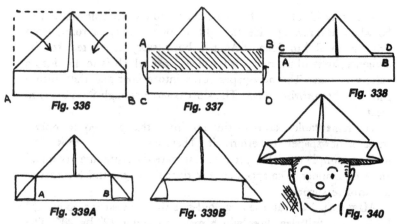

Fig. 336   Fig. 337   Fig. 338

Fig. 339A   Fig. 339B   Fig. 340

"Then he thought of the rough seas when the weather turned cold and decided he didn't want that." Remove the hat. Bring AC and BD together, Figure 341. The hat will fold flat, Figure 342A. Fold flap C down flat under A, Figure 342B. Then fold A down flat on top of it, Figure 342C. Do the same with D and B in back. Open out the hat, Figure 343, and put it on.

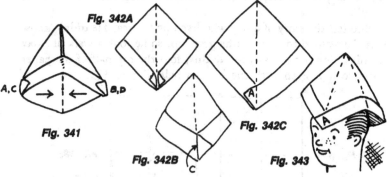

Fig. 342A   Fig. 341   Fig. 342B   Fig. 342C   Fig. 343

"He thought he might become a soldier, but he didn't want to be shot at." Take off the hat and fold it flat. Fold the front layer up on the dotted line as shown by the arrow in Figure 344. This gives you the fireman's hat of Figure 345. Put on the hat. "He thought he could become a fireman and save people from burning buildings. But the flames might burn him. No, he didn't think he'd want to be a fireman."

Take off the hat. Fold B up in the direction of the arrow in Figure 346. Put on the hat, Figure 347. "He could be Robin

Hood and steal from the rich to give money to the poor. But he might get caught and put in jail. No, he didn't want to be Robin Hood."

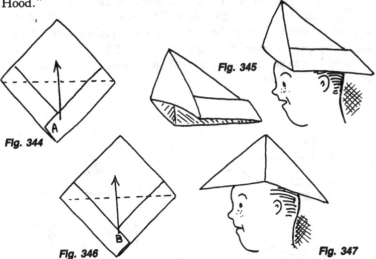

Fig. 344
Fig. 345
Fig. 346
Fig. 347

Take off the hat. Fold in the ends, Figure 348. The hat will then look like Figure 349. Grasp A, C in your left hand and B, D in your right hand. Pull them in opposite directions. The newspaper will open out into the boat of Figure 350.

"By this time he reached the water and saw a boat out at sea. The boat hit a rock. The front fell off." Tear off the prow, Figure 351.

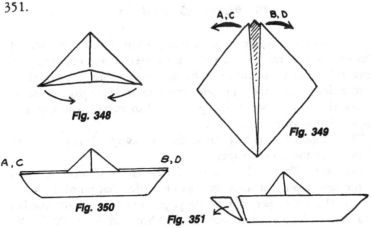

Fig. 348
Fig. 349
Fig. 350
Fig. 351

"The back fell off." Tear off the stern, Figure 352.

"It became dark; there was thunder. A streak of lightning tore off the top." Tear off the top of the boat, Figure 353.

"The ship started to go down. The boy rescued all of the passengers. For his reward he was given the captain's shirt." Open the newspaper to reveal the shirt of Figure 354.

To add color you can use the comic section of the newspaper, or gift-wrapping paper.

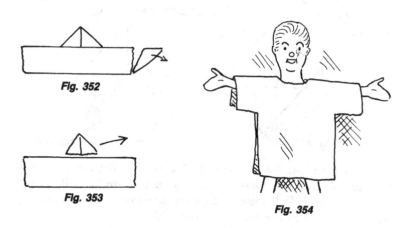

Fig. 352

Fig. 353

Fig. 354

79 ALMANAC AFFINITY

News passes from the pages of daily newspapers to the pages of almanacs where names and dates are preserved for posterity. To show this affinity, the magician has the spectator remove any sheet from a daily newspaper. He adds together the four page numbers on the sheet. Without revealing the total to anyone, the spectator opens to that page in an almanac.

The magician, standing some distance away, then reveals the contents of the chosen page.

METHOD: The total is forced. Whatever the number of pages in the newspaper, the force total will be twice that number plus 2. If, say, the newspaper contains 48 pages, to find the force number you would double 48 to obtain 96, then add 2 to obtain 98.

Beforehand, open the almanac to page 98 and familiarize yourself with the contents of that page.

To present the trick, give the newspaper to one spectator, the almanac to another. Explain that the almanac contains names, dates and events that originally appeared in daily newspapers. There is an affinity between the two that you'd like to demonstrate.

Have the newspaper opened out flat. The loose sheets can be scattered about on the table. Have the spectator pick one sheet. It will contain four page numbers. Tell him to add them together. The addition can be speeded by using a pocket calculator.

He then opens the almanac to the page represented by the total. If a 48-page newspaper was used, he must open the almanac to page 98. Proceed to reveal the contents of the page.

There is a way to prevent any thought of a force. Purchase two copies of today's paper and one of yesterday's paper. Make sure today's paper contains a different number of pages from yesterday's. We will assume that today's paper has 48 pages and yesterday's paper has 56 pages.

Remove the front sheet of yesterday's paper. This sheet contains pages 1, 2, 55, 56. Discard this sheet since it won't be used. Take the front sheet from one of today's papers. Discard the balance of this newspaper. Use the front sheet from this newspaper as the front sheet of yesterday's newspaper.

The result is that you will have one complete copy of today's newspaper plus one copy of yesterday's paper that has today's front sheet. To the audience it appears as if you have two copies of today's newspaper. Although the newspapers appear identical, they contain different numbers of pages.

Hand the genuine copy of today's paper to one spectator. Hand the prepared copy of yesterday's paper to another spectator. Have each remove a full sheet. Each person adds together the four page numbers and remembers the total.

The spectator with the 48-page newspaper will arrive at the force total of 98. The spectator with the 56-page newspaper will arrive at the force total of 114.

Each spectator opens the almanac to the page represented by his total. You reveal the contents of the chosen pages without asking a single question because beforehand you familiarized yourself with the contents of pages 98 and 114.

Try to tie in the revelations with current events. If, for example, page 98 contains census figures, remark that the newspapers recently carried stories about population shifts brought to light by recent census studies.

In the version above the spectators arrive at different totals even though they use copies of apparently the same newspaper. This gets away from the idea of a force.

80   MIRROR, MIRROR

To perform this astonishing routine you require a long strip of paper, a pencil and an ornamental mirror. The long strip of paper looks like the one shown in Figure 355 except that the top and bottom sections are left blank.

The spectator's first name is printed on the top section of the paper. His last name is printed on the bottom section. The paper now looks exactly as shown in Figure 355. The paper is held up to a mirror. The magician remarks that mirrors have the ability to reverse words. When the paper is seen by the spectator, his name is indeed reversed. It looks like Figure 356. His first name is now at the bottom of the paper and his last name at the top.

Only one strip of paper is used.

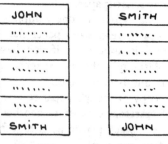

Fig. 355   **Fig. 356**

METHOD: This trick was devised by Jacob Daley and L. Vosburgh Lyons. Divide a long strip of paper into ten segments. An easy way to do this is to fold the paper in half four times. When opened out it will contain 16 segments. Trim off six segments. You will be left with a strip of ten segments. Crease each section both ways. Then draw lines across the folds on both sides of the paper. Fill in the names shown in Figure 357. Note that these words will look the same when viewed in a mirror. The top and bottom sections are left blank.

Turn over the strip end for end (top to bottom) and fill in the strip as shown in Figure 358. All ten segments are filled in. Use block letters on both sides so that the words will look unchanged when viewed in a mirror.

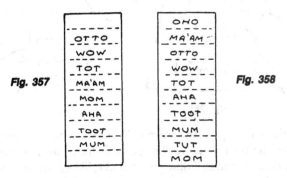

Fig. 357   **Fig. 358**

When this has been done, fold over the blank sections as shown in Figure 359. Hold them in place with your thumbs, Figure 360. With the paper in this condition, show it on both sides. Point out that the end sections are blank but that the other sections contain words which look the same whether viewed straight on or reflected in a mirror.

Fig. 359   **Fig. 360**

Place the strip on a pad. Ask the spectator for his name or for the name of one of his friends. Jot it down, first name at the top of the strip, last name at the bottom, Figure 361. Put the pencil aside. Keep the top segment and the bottom segment in place with your thumbs as you display the writing. Point out that the spectator's first name is at the top and his last name at the bottom.

With the right hand remove the mirror from the pocket. It should be in a case or an envelope. Ask the spectator to remove it from the case. This takes attention away from you, allowing you to flip over the end sections of the strip with your thumbs as shown in Figure 362.

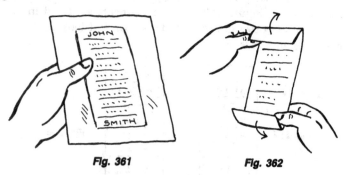

Fig. 361   **Fig. 362**

Hold the strip up to the mirror. The side with the spectator's name faces the mirror. Have the spectator look into the mirror to see the reflected image. Point out that the list of words looks the same, but that his name is reversed.

It will slowly dawn on him that his first and last names have somehow changed places.

81 MAGIC WITH *PAPER MAGIC*

The magician writes a double prediction and places it aside. The spectator is asked to shuffle a packet of cards. He then deals it out into four heaps and chooses one heap. The lowest card in the heap is placed in his pocket.

Of the remaining two cards, he subtracts the lowest from the highest. For example, if he holds a 6-spot and a 10-spot, he subtracts 6 from 10 and gets 4. The spectator opens *Self-Working Paper Magic* to the first page of any chapter and notes the fourth word in the chapter. That word might be "tricks." The first prediction is opened. It correctly predicts that "tricks" would be chosen.

Then the spectator removes the card from his pocket. It may be a 2-spot. The second prediction is read aloud. It correctly predicts that a 2-spot would be chosen.

METHOD: On top of the deck have the four 2's, followed by the four 6's and then the four 10's. On a slip of paper write, "You will choose 'tricks.'" On a second piece of paper write, "You will choose a 2." Each slip is folded and placed in full view.

Hand the spectator the top four cards of the deck. There are the 2's. Ask him to shuffle them face down. After the shuffle, take the four 2's and place them face down on the table. Hand him the four 6's for shuffling. After these cards have been mixed, place them face down on top of the 2's. Then have the 10's mixed. After they are shuffled, place them face down on top of the 6's. The spectator should not see the faces of the cards during the mixing process.

Have him cut the packet and complete the cut. He can give the packet any number of straight cuts. Then have him deal the packet into four heaps, a card at a time to each heap until he has dealt out all 12 cards. Unknown to the spectator, each three-card heap will contain a 2, a 6 and a 10.

He chooses any heap. Take the remaining three heaps and shuffle them back into the deck to destroy the evidence. Then have him pocket the lowest-value card in his heap. It will be a 2-spot. Of the two remaining cards he subtracts the smallest from the largest. The result must be 4.

The spectator opens *Self-Working Paper Magic* to the first page of any chapter. He can even open the book to the Introduction. Since his result is 4, have him note the fourth word in the chapter. That word will always be "tricks."

Hand him the first prediction to show you correctly predicted the word. Then have him remove the card from his pocket. The second prediction correctly indicates he would pick a 2-spot.

A CATALOG OF SELECTED
DOVER BOOKS
IN ALL FIELDS OF INTEREST

A CATALOG OF SELECTED DOVER BOOKS IN ALL FIELDS OF INTEREST

100 BEST-LOVED POEMS, Edited by Philip Smith. "The Passionate Shepherd to His Love," "Shall I compare thee to a summer's day?" "Death, be not proud," "The Raven," "The Road Not Taken," plus works by Blake, Wordsworth, Byron, Shelley, Keats, many others. 96pp. $5\frac{3}{16}$ x $8\frac{1}{4}$. 0-486-28553-7

100 SMALL HOUSES OF THE THIRTIES, Brown-Blodgett Company. Exterior photographs and floor plans for 100 charming structures. Illustrations of models accompanied by descriptions of interiors, color schemes, closet space, and other amenities. 200 illustrations. 112pp. $8\frac{3}{8}$ x 11. 0-486-44131-8

1000 TURN-OF-THE-CENTURY HOUSES: With Illustrations and Floor Plans, Herbert C. Chivers. Reproduced from a rare edition, this showcase of homes ranges from cottages and bungalows to sprawling mansions. Each house is meticulously illustrated and accompanied by complete floor plans. 256pp. $9\frac{3}{8}$ x $12\frac{1}{4}$. 0-486-45596-3

101 GREAT AMERICAN POEMS, Edited by The American Poetry & Literacy Project. Rich treasury of verse from the 19th and 20th centuries includes works by Edgar Allan Poe, Robert Frost, Walt Whitman, Langston Hughes, Emily Dickinson, T. S. Eliot, other notables. 96pp. $5\frac{3}{16}$ x $8\frac{1}{4}$. 0-486-40158-8

101 GREAT SAMURAI PRINTS, Utagawa Kuniyoshi. Kuniyoshi was a master of the warrior woodblock print — and these 18th-century illustrations represent the pinnacle of his craft. Full-color portraits of renowned Japanese samurais pulse with movement, passion, and remarkably fine detail. 112pp. $8\frac{3}{8}$ x 11. 0-486-46523-3

ABC OF BALLET, Janet Grosser. Clearly worded, abundantly illustrated little guide defines basic ballet-related terms: arabesque, battement, pas de chat, relevé, sissonne, many others. Pronunciation guide included. Excellent primer. 48pp. $4\frac{3}{16}$ x $5\frac{3}{4}$. 0-486-40871-X

ACCESSORIES OF DRESS: An Illustrated Encyclopedia, Katherine Lester and Bess Viola Oerke. Illustrations of hats, veils, wigs, cravats, shawls, shoes, gloves, and other accessories enhance an engaging commentary that reveals the humor and charm of the many-sided story of accessorized apparel. 644 figures and 59 plates. 608pp. $6\frac{1}{8}$ x $9\frac{1}{4}$. 0-486-43378-1

ADVENTURES OF HUCKLEBERRY FINN, Mark Twain. Join Huck and Jim as their boyhood adventures along the Mississippi River lead them into a world of excitement, danger, and self-discovery. Humorous narrative, lyrical descriptions of the Mississippi valley, and memorable characters. 224pp. $5\frac{3}{16}$ x $8\frac{1}{4}$. 0-486-28061-6

ALICE STARMORE'S BOOK OF FAIR ISLE KNITTING, Alice Starmore. A noted designer from the region of Scotland's Fair Isle explores the history and techniques of this distinctive, stranded-color knitting style and provides copious illustrated instructions for 14 original knitwear designs. 208pp. $8\frac{3}{8}$ x $10\frac{7}{8}$. 0-486-47218-3

Browse over 9,000 books at www.doverpublications.com

CATALOG OF DOVER BOOKS

ALICE'S ADVENTURES IN WONDERLAND, Lewis Carroll. Beloved classic about a little girl lost in a topsy-turvy land and her encounters with the White Rabbit, March Hare, Mad Hatter, Cheshire Cat, and other delightfully improbable characters. 42 illustrations by Sir John Tenniel. 96pp. 5¾₆ x 8¼.   0-486-27543-4

AMERICA'S LIGHTHOUSES: An Illustrated History, Francis Ross Holland. Profusely illustrated fact-filled survey of American lighthouses since 1716. Over 200 stations — East, Gulf, and West coasts, Great Lakes, Hawaii, Alaska, Puerto Rico, the Virgin Islands, and the Mississippi and St. Lawrence Rivers. 240pp. 8 x 10¾.
0-486-25576-X

AN ENCYCLOPEDIA OF THE VIOLIN, Alberto Bachmann. Translated by Frederick H. Martens. Introduction by Eugene Ysaye. First published in 1925, this renowned reference remains unsurpassed as a source of essential information, from construction and evolution to repertoire and technique. Includes a glossary and 73 illustrations. 496pp. 6⅛ x 9¼.   0-486-46618-3

ANIMALS: 1,419 Copyright-Free Illustrations of Mammals, Birds, Fish, Insects, etc., Selected by Jim Harter. Selected for its visual impact and ease of use, this outstanding collection of wood engravings presents over 1,000 species of animals in extremely lifelike poses. Includes mammals, birds, reptiles, amphibians, fish, insects, and other invertebrates. 284pp. 9 x 12.   0-486-23766-4

THE ANNALS, Tacitus. Translated by Alfred John Church and William Jackson Brodribb. This vital chronicle of Imperial Rome, written by the era's great historian, spans A.D. 14-68 and paints incisive psychological portraits of major figures, from Tiberius to Nero. 416pp. 5¾₆ x 8¼.   0-486-45236-0

ANTIGONE, Sophocles. Filled with passionate speeches and sensitive probing of moral and philosophical issues, this powerful and often-performed Greek drama reveals the grim fate that befalls the children of Oedipus. Footnotes. 64pp. 5¾₆ x 8 ¼.   0-486-27804-2

ART DECO DECORATIVE PATTERNS IN FULL COLOR, Christian Stoll. Reprinted from a rare 1910 portfolio, 160 sensuous and exotic images depict a breathtaking array of florals, geometrics, and abstracts — all elegant in their stark simplicity. 64pp. 8⅜ x 11.   0-486-44862-2

THE ARTHUR RACKHAM TREASURY: 86 Full-Color Illustrations, Arthur Rackham. Selected and Edited by Jeff A. Menges. A stunning treasury of 86 full-page plates span the famed English artist's career, from *Rip Van Winkle* (1905) to masterworks such as *Undine, A Midsummer Night's Dream,* and *Wind in the Willows* (1939). 96pp. 8⅜ x 11.
0-486-44685-9

THE AUTHENTIC GILBERT & SULLIVAN SONGBOOK, W. S. Gilbert and A. S. Sullivan. The most comprehensive collection available, this songbook includes selections from every one of Gilbert and Sullivan's light operas. Ninety-two numbers are presented uncut and unedited, and in their original keys. 410pp. 9 x 12.
0-486-23482-7

THE AWAKENING, Kate Chopin. First published in 1899, this controversial novel of a New Orleans wife's search for love outside a stifling marriage shocked readers. Today, it remains a first-rate narrative with superb characterization. New introductory Note. 128pp. 5¾₆ x 8¼.   0-486-27786-0

BASIC DRAWING, Louis Priscilla. Beginning with perspective, this commonsense manual progresses to the figure in movement, light and shade, anatomy, drapery, composition, trees and landscape, and outdoor sketching. Black-and-white illustrations throughout. 128pp. 8⅜ x 11.   0-486-45815-6

Browse over 9,000 books at www.doverpublications.com

THE BATTLES THAT CHANGED HISTORY, Fletcher Pratt. Historian profiles 16 crucial conflicts, ancient to modern, that changed the course of Western civilization. Gripping accounts of battles led by Alexander the Great, Joan of Arc, Ulysses S. Grant, other commanders. 27 maps. 352pp. 5⅜ x 8½. 0-486-41129-X

BEETHOVEN'S LETTERS, Ludwig van Beethoven. Edited by Dr. A. C. Kalischer. Features 457 letters to fellow musicians, friends, greats, patrons, and literary men. Reveals musical thoughts, quirks of personality, insights, and daily events. Includes 15 plates. 410pp. 5⅜ x 8½. 0-486-22769-3

BERNICE BOBS HER HAIR AND OTHER STORIES, F. Scott Fitzgerald. This brilliant anthology includes 6 of Fitzgerald's most popular stories: "The Diamond as Big as the Ritz," the title tale, "The Offshore Pirate," "The Ice Palace," "The Jelly Bean," and "May Day." 176pp. 5⅜ x 8½. 0-486-47049-0

BESLER'S BOOK OF FLOWERS AND PLANTS: 73 Full-Color Plates from Hortus Eystettensis, 1613, Basilius Besler. Here is a selection of magnificent plates from the *Hortus Eystettensis,* which vividly illustrated and identified the plants, flowers, and trees that thrived in the legendary German garden at Eichstätt. 80pp. 8⅜ x 11.
0-486-46005-3

THE BOOK OF KELLS, Edited by Blanche Cirker. Painstakingly reproduced from a rare facsimile edition, this volume contains full-page decorations, portraits, illustrations, plus a sampling of textual leaves with exquisite calligraphy and ornamentation. 32 full-color illustrations. 32pp. 9⅜ x 12¼. 0-486-24345-1

THE BOOK OF THE CROSSBOW: With an Additional Section on Catapults and Other Siege Engines, Ralph Payne-Gallwey. Fascinating study traces history and use of crossbow as military and sporting weapon, from Middle Ages to modern times. Also covers related weapons: balistas, catapults, Turkish bows, more. Over 240 illustrations. 400pp. 7¼ x 10⅛. 0-486-28720-3

THE BUNGALOW BOOK: Floor Plans and Photos of 112 Houses, 1910, Henry L. Wilson. Here are 112 of the most popular and economic blueprints of the early 20th century — plus an illustration or photograph of each completed house. A wonderful time capsule that still offers a wealth of valuable insights. 160pp. 8⅜ x 11.
0-486-45104-6

THE CALL OF THE WILD, Jack London. A classic novel of adventure, drawn from London's own experiences as a Klondike adventurer, relating the story of a heroic dog caught in the brutal life of the Alaska Gold Rush. Note. 64pp. 5³⁄₁₆ x 8¼.
0-486-26472-6

CANDIDE, Voltaire. Edited by Francois-Marie Arouet. One of the world's great satires since its first publication in 1759. Witty, caustic skewering of romance, science, philosophy, religion, government — nearly all human ideals and institutions. 112pp. 5³⁄₁₆ x 8¼. 0-486-26689-3

CELEBRATED IN THEIR TIME: Photographic Portraits from the George Grantham Bain Collection, Edited by Amy Pastan. With an Introduction by Michael Carlebach. Remarkable portrait gallery features 112 rare images of Albert Einstein, Charlie Chaplin, the Wright Brothers, Henry Ford, and other luminaries from the worlds of politics, art, entertainment, and industry. 128pp. 8⅜ x 11. 0-486-46754-6

CHARIOTS FOR APOLLO: The NASA History of Manned Lunar Spacecraft to 1969, Courtney G. Brooks, James M. Grimwood, and Loyd S. Swenson, Jr. This illustrated history by a trio of experts is the definitive reference on the Apollo spacecraft and lunar modules. It traces the vehicles' design, development, and operation in space. More than 100 photographs and illustrations. 576pp. 6¾ x 9¼. 0-486-46756-2

A CHRISTMAS CAROL, Charles Dickens. This engrossing tale relates Ebenezer Scrooge's ghostly journeys through Christmases past, present, and future and his ultimate transformation from a harsh and grasping old miser to a charitable and compassionate human being. 80pp. 5³⁄₁₆ x 8¼. 0-486-26865-9

COMMON SENSE, Thomas Paine. First published in January of 1776, this highly influential landmark document clearly and persuasively argued for American separation from Great Britain and paved the way for the Declaration of Independence. 64pp. 5³⁄₁₆ x 8¼. 0-486-29602-4

THE COMPLETE SHORT STORIES OF OSCAR WILDE, Oscar Wilde. Complete texts of "The Happy Prince and Other Tales," "A House of Pomegranates," "Lord Arthur Savile's Crime and Other Stories," "Poems in Prose," and "The Portrait of Mr. W. H." 208pp. 5³⁄₁₆ x 8¼. 0-486-45216-6

COMPLETE SONNETS, William Shakespeare. Over 150 exquisite poems deal with love, friendship, the tyranny of time, beauty's evanescence, death, and other themes in language of remarkable power, precision, and beauty. Glossary of archaic terms. 80pp. 5³⁄₁₆ x 8¼. 0-486-26686-9

THE COUNT OF MONTE CRISTO: Abridged Edition, Alexandre Dumas. Falsely accused of treason, Edmond Dantès is imprisoned in the bleak Chateau d'If. After a hair-raising escape, he launches an elaborate plot to extract a bitter revenge against those who betrayed him. 448pp. 5³⁄₁₆ x 8¼. 0-486-45643-9

CRAFTSMAN BUNGALOWS: Designs from the Pacific Northwest, Yoho & Merritt. This reprint of a rare catalog, showcasing the charming simplicity and cozy style of Craftsman bungalows, is filled with photos of completed homes, plus floor plans and estimated costs. An indispensable resource for architects, historians, and illustrators. 112pp. 10 x 7. 0-486-46875-5

CRAFTSMAN BUNGALOWS: 59 Homes from "The Craftsman," Edited by Gustav Stickley. Best and most attractive designs from Arts and Crafts Movement publication — 1903–1916 — includes sketches, photographs of homes, floor plans, descriptive text. 128pp. 8¼ x 11. 0-486-25829-7

CRIME AND PUNISHMENT, Fyodor Dostoyevsky. Translated by Constance Garnett. Supreme masterpiece tells the story of Raskolnikov, a student tormented by his own thoughts after he murders an old woman. Overwhelmed by guilt and terror, he confesses and goes to prison. 480pp. 5³⁄₁₆ x 8¼. 0-486-41587-2

THE DECLARATION OF INDEPENDENCE AND OTHER GREAT DOCUMENTS OF AMERICAN HISTORY: 1775-1865, Edited by John Grafton. Thirteen compelling and influential documents: Henry's "Give Me Liberty or Give Me Death," Declaration of Independence, The Constitution, Washington's First Inaugural Address, The Monroe Doctrine, The Emancipation Proclamation, Gettysburg Address, more. 64pp. 5³⁄₁₆ x 8¼. 0-486-41124-9

THE DESERT AND THE SOWN: Travels in Palestine and Syria, Gertrude Bell. "The female Lawrence of Arabia," Gertrude Bell wrote captivating, perceptive accounts of her travels in the Middle East. This intriguing narrative, accompanied by 160 photos, traces her 1905 sojourn in Lebanon, Syria, and Palestine. 368pp. 5⅜ x 8½. 0-486-46876-3

A DOLL'S HOUSE, Henrik Ibsen. Ibsen's best-known play displays his genius for realistic prose drama. An expression of women's rights, the play climaxes when the central character, Nora, rejects a smothering marriage and life in "a doll's house." 80pp. 5³⁄₁₆ x 8¼. 0-486-27062-9

DOOMED SHIPS: Great Ocean Liner Disasters, William H. Miller, Jr. Nearly 200 photographs, many from private collections, highlight tales of some of the vessels whose pleasure cruises ended in catastrophe: the *Morro Castle, Normandie, Andrea Doria, Europa,* and many others. 128pp. 8⅞ x 11¾.   0-486-45366-9

THE DORÉ BIBLE ILLUSTRATIONS, Gustave Doré. Detailed plates from the Bible: the Creation scenes, Adam and Eve, horrifying visions of the Flood, the battle sequences with their monumental crowds, depictions of the life of Jesus, 241 plates in all. 241pp. 9 x 12.   0-486-23004-X

DRAWING DRAPERY FROM HEAD TO TOE, Cliff Young. Expert guidance on how to draw shirts, pants, skirts, gloves, hats, and coats on the human figure, including folds in relation to the body, pull and crush, action folds, creases, more. Over 200 drawings. 48pp. 8¼ x 11.   0-486-45591-2

DUBLINERS, James Joyce. A fine and accessible introduction to the work of one of the 20th century's most influential writers, this collection features 15 tales, including a masterpiece of the short-story genre, "The Dead." 160pp. 5³⁄₁₆ x 8¼.

0-486-26870-5

EASY-TO-MAKE POP-UPS, Joan Irvine. Illustrated by Barbara Reid. Dozens of wonderful ideas for three-dimensional paper fun — from holiday greeting cards with moving parts to a pop-up menagerie. Easy-to-follow, illustrated instructions for more than 30 projects. 299 black-and-white illustrations. 96pp. 8⅜ x 11.

0-486-44622-0

EASY-TO-MAKE STORYBOOK DOLLS: A "Novel" Approach to Cloth Dollmaking, Sherralyn St. Clair. Favorite fictional characters come alive in this unique beginner's dollmaking guide. Includes patterns for Pollyanna, Dorothy from *The Wonderful Wizard of Oz,* Mary of *The Secret Garden,* plus easy-to-follow instructions, 263 black-and-white illustrations, and an 8-page color insert. 112pp. 8¼ x 11.   0-486-47360-0

EINSTEIN'S ESSAYS IN SCIENCE, Albert Einstein. Speeches and essays in accessible, everyday language profile influential physicists such as Niels Bohr and Isaac Newton. They also explore areas of physics to which the author made major contributions. 128pp. 5 x 8.   0-486-47011-3

EL DORADO: Further Adventures of the Scarlet Pimpernel, Baroness Orczy. A popular sequel to *The Scarlet Pimpernel,* this suspenseful story recounts the Pimpernel's attempts to rescue the Dauphin from imprisonment during the French Revolution. An irresistible blend of intrigue, period detail, and vibrant characterizations. 352pp. 5³⁄₁₆ x 8¼.   0-486-44026-5

ELEGANT SMALL HOMES OF THE TWENTIES: 99 Designs from a Competition, Chicago Tribune. Nearly 100 designs for five- and six-room houses feature New England and Southern colonials, Normandy cottages, stately Italianate dwellings, and other fascinating snapshots of American domestic architecture of the 1920s. 112pp. 9 x 12.   0-486-46910-7

THE ELEMENTS OF STYLE: The Original Edition, William Strunk, Jr. This is the book that generations of writers have relied upon for timeless advice on grammar, diction, syntax, and other essentials. In concise terms, it identifies the principal requirements of proper style and common errors. 64pp. 5⅜ x 8½.   0-486-44798-7

THE ELUSIVE PIMPERNEL, Baroness Orczy. Robespierre's revolutionaries find their wicked schemes thwarted by the heroic Pimpernel — Sir Percival Blakeney. In this thrilling sequel, Chauvelin devises a plot to eliminate the Pimpernel and his wife. 272pp. 5³⁄₁₆ x 8¼.   0-486-45464-9

AN ENCYCLOPEDIA OF BATTLES: Accounts of Over 1,560 Battles from 1479 B.C. to the Present, David Eggenberger. Essential details of every major battle in recorded history from the first battle of Megiddo in 1479 B.C. to Grenada in 1984. List of battle maps. 99 illustrations. 544pp. 6½ x 9¼. 0-486-24913-1

ENCYCLOPEDIA OF EMBROIDERY STITCHES, INCLUDING CREWEL, Marion Nichols. Precise explanations and instructions, clearly illustrated, on how to work chain, back, cross, knotted, woven stitches, and many more — 178 in all, including Cable Outline, Whipped Satin, and Eyelet Buttonhole. Over 1400 illustrations. 219pp. 8⅜ x 11¼. 0-486-22929-7

ENTER JEEVES: 15 Early Stories, P. G. Wodehouse. Splendid collection contains first 8 stories featuring Bertie Wooster, the deliciously dim aristocrat and Jeeves, his brainy, imperturbable manservant. Also, the complete Reggie Pepper (Bertie's prototype) series. 288pp. 5⅜ x 8½. 0-486-29717-9

ERIC SLOANE'S AMERICA: Paintings in Oil, Michael Wigley. With a Foreword by Mimi Sloane. Eric Sloane's evocative oils of America's landscape and material culture shimmer with immense historical and nostalgic appeal. This original hardcover collection gathers nearly a hundred of his finest paintings, with subjects ranging from New England to the American Southwest. 128pp. 10⅝ x 9. 0-486-46525-X

ETHAN FROME, Edith Wharton. Classic story of wasted lives, set against a bleak New England background. Superbly delineated characters in a hauntingly grim tale of thwarted love. Considered by many to be Wharton's masterpiece. 96pp. 5³⁄₁₆ x 8 ¼. 0-486-26690-7

THE EVERLASTING MAN, G. K. Chesterton. Chesterton's view of Christianity — as a blend of philosophy and mythology, satisfying intellect and spirit — applies to his brilliant book, which appeals to readers' heads as well as their hearts. 288pp. 5⅜ x 8½. 0-486-46036-3

THE FIELD AND FOREST HANDY BOOK, Daniel Beard. Written by a co-founder of the Boy Scouts, this appealing guide offers illustrated instructions for building kites, birdhouses, boats, igloos, and other fun projects, plus numerous helpful tips for campers. 448pp. 5³⁄₁₆ x 8¼. 0-486-46191-2

FINDING YOUR WAY WITHOUT MAP OR COMPASS, Harold Gatty. Useful, instructive manual shows would-be explorers, hikers, bikers, scouts, sailors, and survivalists how to find their way outdoors by observing animals, weather patterns, shifting sands, and other elements of nature. 288pp. 5⅜ x 8½. 0-486-40613-X

FIRST FRENCH READER: A Beginner's Dual-Language Book, Edited and Translated by Stanley Appelbaum. This anthology introduces 50 legendary writers — Voltaire, Balzac, Baudelaire, Proust, more — through passages from *The Red and the Black, Les Misérables, Madame Bovary,* and other classics. Original French text plus English translation on facing pages. 240pp. 5⅜ x 8½. 0-486-46178-5

FIRST GERMAN READER: A Beginner's Dual-Language Book, Edited by Harry Steinhauer. Specially chosen for their power to evoke German life and culture, these short, simple readings include poems, stories, essays, and anecdotes by Goethe, Hesse, Heine, Schiller, and others. 224pp. 5⅜ x 8½. 0-486-46179-3

FIRST SPANISH READER: A Beginner's Dual-Language Book, Angel Flores. Delightful stories, other material based on works of Don Juan Manuel, Luis Taboada, Ricardo Palma, other noted writers. Complete faithful English translations on facing pages. Exercises. 176pp. 5⅜ x 8½. 0-486-25810-6

Browse over 9,000 books at www.doverpublications.com

FIVE ACRES AND INDEPENDENCE, Maurice G. Kains. Great back-to-the-land classic explains basics of self-sufficient farming. The one book to get. 95 illustrations. 397pp. 5⅜ x 8½.   0-486-20974-1

FLAGG'S SMALL HOUSES: Their Economic Design and Construction, 1922, Ernest Flagg. Although most famous for his skyscrapers, Flagg was also a proponent of the well-designed single-family dwelling. His classic treatise features innovations that save space, materials, and cost. 526 illustrations. 160pp. 9⅜ x 12¼.
0-486-45197-6

FLATLAND: A Romance of Many Dimensions, Edwin A. Abbott. Classic of science (and mathematical) fiction — charmingly illustrated by the author — describes the adventures of A. Square, a resident of Flatland, in Spaceland (three dimensions), Lineland (one dimension), and Pointland (no dimensions). 96pp. 5³⁄₁₆ x 8¼.
0-486-27263-X

FRANKENSTEIN, Mary Shelley. The story of Victor Frankenstein's monstrous creation and the havoc it caused has enthralled generations of readers and inspired countless writers of horror and suspense. With the author's own 1831 introduction. 176pp. 5³⁄₁₆ x 8¼.   0-486-28211-2

THE GARGOYLE BOOK: 572 Examples from Gothic Architecture, Lester Burbank Bridaham. Dispelling the conventional wisdom that French Gothic architectural flourishes were born of despair or gloom, Bridaham reveals the whimsical nature of these creations and the ingenious artisans who made them. 572 illustrations. 224pp. 8⅜ x 11.   0-486-44754-5

THE GIFT OF THE MAGI AND OTHER SHORT STORIES, O. Henry. Sixteen captivating stories by one of America's most popular storytellers. Included are such classics as "The Gift of the Magi," "The Last Leaf," and "The Ransom of Red Chief." Publisher's Note. 96pp. 5³⁄₁₆ x 8¼.   0-486-27061-0

THE GOETHE TREASURY: Selected Prose and Poetry, Johann Wolfgang von Goethe. Edited, Selected, and with an Introduction by Thomas Mann. In addition to his lyric poetry, Goethe wrote travel sketches, autobiographical studies, essays, letters, and proverbs in rhyme and prose. This collection presents outstanding examples from each genre. 368pp. 5⅜ x 8½.   0-486-44780-4

GREAT EXPECTATIONS, Charles Dickens. Orphaned Pip is apprenticed to the dirty work of the forge but dreams of becoming a gentleman — and one day finds himself in possession of "great expectations." Dickens' finest novel. 400pp. 5³⁄₁₆ x 8¼.
0-486-41586-4

GREAT WRITERS ON THE ART OF FICTION: From Mark Twain to Joyce Carol Oates, Edited by James Daley. An indispensable source of advice and inspiration, this anthology features essays by Henry James, Kate Chopin, Willa Cather, Sinclair Lewis, Jack London, Raymond Chandler, Raymond Carver, Eudora Welty, and Kurt Vonnegut, Jr. 192pp. 5⅜ x 8½.   0-486-45128-3

HAMLET, William Shakespeare. The quintessential Shakespearean tragedy, whose highly charged confrontations and anguished soliloquies probe depths of human feeling rarely sounded in any art. Reprinted from an authoritative British edition complete with illuminating footnotes. 128pp. 5³⁄₁₆ x 8¼.   0-486-27278-8

THE HAUNTED HOUSE, Charles Dickens. A Yuletide gathering in an eerie country retreat provides the backdrop for Dickens and his friends — including Elizabeth Gaskell and Wilkie Collins — who take turns spinning supernatural yarns. 144pp. 5⅜ x 8½.   0-486-46309-5

HEART OF DARKNESS, Joseph Conrad. Dark allegory of a journey up the Congo River and the narrator's encounter with the mysterious Mr. Kurtz. Masterly blend of adventure, character study, psychological penetration. For many, Conrad's finest, most enigmatic story. 80pp. $5\frac{3}{16}$ x $8\frac{1}{4}$. 0-486-26464-5

HENSON AT THE NORTH POLE, Matthew A. Henson. This thrilling memoir by the heroic African-American who was Peary's companion through two decades of Arctic exploration recounts a tale of danger, courage, and determination. "Fascinating and exciting." — *Commonweal.* 128pp. $5\frac{3}{8}$ x $8\frac{1}{2}$. 0-486-45472-X

HISTORIC COSTUMES AND HOW TO MAKE THEM, Mary Fernald and E. Shenton. Practical, informative guidebook shows how to create everything from short tunics worn by Saxon men in the fifth century to a lady's bustle dress of the late 1800s. 81 illustrations. 176pp. $5\frac{3}{8}$ x $8\frac{1}{2}$. 0-486-44906-8

THE HOUND OF THE BASKERVILLES, Arthur Conan Doyle. A deadly curse in the form of a legendary ferocious beast continues to claim its victims from the Baskerville family until Holmes and Watson intervene. Often called the best detective story ever written. 128pp. $5\frac{3}{16}$ x $8\frac{1}{4}$. 0-486-28214-7

THE HOUSE BEHIND THE CEDARS, Charles W. Chesnutt. Originally published in 1900, this groundbreaking novel by a distinguished African-American author recounts the drama of a brother and sister who "pass for white" during the dangerous days of Reconstruction. 208pp. $5\frac{3}{8}$ x $8\frac{1}{2}$. 0-486-46144-0

THE HUMAN FIGURE IN MOTION, Eadweard Muybridge. The 4,789 photographs in this definitive selection show the human figure — models almost all undraped — engaged in over 160 different types of action: running, climbing stairs, etc. 390pp. $7\frac{7}{8}$ x $10\frac{5}{8}$. 0-486-20204-6

THE IMPORTANCE OF BEING EARNEST, Oscar Wilde. Wilde's witty and buoyant comedy of manners, filled with some of literature's most famous epigrams, reprinted from an authoritative British edition. Considered Wilde's most perfect work. 64pp. $5\frac{3}{16}$ x $8\frac{1}{4}$. 0-486-26478-5

THE INFERNO, Dante Alighieri. Translated and with notes by Henry Wadsworth Longfellow. The first stop on Dante's famous journey from Hell to Purgatory to Paradise, this 14th-century allegorical poem blends vivid and shocking imagery with graceful lyricism. Translated by the beloved 19th-century poet, Henry Wadsworth Longfellow. 256pp. $5\frac{3}{16}$ x $8\frac{1}{4}$. 0-486-44288-8

JANE EYRE, Charlotte Brontë. Written in 1847, *Jane Eyre* tells the tale of an orphan girl's progress from the custody of cruel relatives to an oppressive boarding school and its culmination in a troubled career as a governess. 448pp. $5\frac{3}{16}$ x $8\frac{1}{4}$. 0-486-42449-9

JAPANESE WOODBLOCK FLOWER PRINTS, Tanigami Kônan. Extraordinary collection of Japanese woodblock prints by a well-known artist features 120 plates in brilliant color. Realistic images from a rare edition include daffodils, tulips, and other familiar and unusual flowers. 128pp. 11 x $8\frac{1}{4}$. 0-486-46442-3

JEWELRY MAKING AND DESIGN, Augustus F. Rose and Antonio Cirino. Professional secrets of jewelry making are revealed in a thorough, practical guide. Over 200 illustrations. 306pp. $5\frac{3}{8}$ x $8\frac{1}{2}$. 0-486-21750-7

JULIUS CAESAR, William Shakespeare. Great tragedy based on Plutarch's account of the lives of Brutus, Julius Caesar and Mark Antony. Evil plotting, ringing oratory, high tragedy with Shakespeare's incomparable insight, dramatic power. Explanatory footnotes. 96pp. $5\frac{3}{16}$ x $8\frac{1}{4}$. 0-486-26876-4

THE JUNGLE, Upton Sinclair. 1906 bestseller shockingly reveals intolerable labor practices and working conditions in the Chicago stockyards as it tells the grim story of a Slavic family that emigrates to America full of optimism but soon faces despair. 320pp. 5³⁄₁₆ x 8¼. 0-486-41923-1

THE KINGDOM OF GOD IS WITHIN YOU, Leo Tolstoy. The soul-searching book that inspired Gandhi to embrace the concept of passive resistance, Tolstoy's 1894 polemic clearly outlines a radical, well-reasoned revision of traditional Christian thinking. 352pp. 5³⁄₁₆ x 8¼. 0-486-45138-0

THE LADY OR THE TIGER?: and Other Logic Puzzles, Raymond M. Smullyan. Created by a renowned puzzle master, these whimsically themed challenges involve paradoxes about probability, time, and change; metapuzzles; and self-referentiality. Nineteen chapters advance in difficulty from relatively simple to highly complex. 1982 edition. 240pp. 5⅜ x 8½. 0-486-47027-X

LEAVES OF GRASS: The Original 1855 Edition, Walt Whitman. Whitman's immortal collection includes some of the greatest poems of modern times, including his masterpiece, "Song of Myself." Shattering standard conventions, it stands as an unabashed celebration of body and nature. 128pp. 5³⁄₁₆ x 8¼. 0-486-45676-5

LES MISÉRABLES, Victor Hugo. Translated by Charles E. Wilbour. Abridged by James K. Robinson. A convict's heroic struggle for justice and redemption plays out against a fiery backdrop of the Napoleonic wars. This edition features the excellent original translation and a sensitive abridgment. 304pp. 6⅛ x 9¼. 0-486-45789-3

LILITH: A Romance, George MacDonald. In this novel by the father of fantasy literature, a man travels through time to meet Adam and Eve and to explore humanity's fall from grace and ultimate redemption. 240pp. 5⅜ x 8½. 0-486-46818-6

THE LOST LANGUAGE OF SYMBOLISM, Harold Bayley. This remarkable book reveals the hidden meaning behind familiar images and words, from the origins of Santa Claus to the fleur-de-lys, drawing from mythology, folklore, religious texts, and fairy tales. 1,418 illustrations. 784pp. 5⅜ x 8½. 0-486-44787-1

MACBETH, William Shakespeare. A Scottish nobleman murders the king in order to succeed to the throne. Tortured by his conscience and fearful of discovery, he becomes tangled in a web of treachery and deceit that ultimately spells his doom. 96pp. 5³⁄₁₆ x 8¼. 0-486-27802-6

MAKING AUTHENTIC CRAFTSMAN FURNITURE: Instructions and Plans for 62 Projects, Gustav Stickley. Make authentic reproductions of handsome, functional, durable furniture: tables, chairs, wall cabinets, desks, a hall tree, and more. Construction plans with drawings, schematics, dimensions, and lumber specs reprinted from 1900s The Craftsman magazine. 128pp. 8⅛ x 11. 0-486-25000-8

MATHEMATICS FOR THE NONMATHEMATICIAN, Morris Kline. Erudite and entertaining overview follows development of mathematics from ancient Greeks to present. Topics include logic and mathematics, the fundamental concept, differential calculus, probability theory, much more. Exercises and problems. 641pp. 5⅜ x 8½. 0-486-24823-2

MEMOIRS OF AN ARABIAN PRINCESS FROM ZANZIBAR, Emily Ruete. This 19th-century autobiography offers a rare inside look at the society surrounding a sultan's palace. A real-life princess in exile recalls her vanished world of harems, slave trading, and court intrigues. 288pp. 5⅜ x 8½. 0-486-47121-7

THE METAMORPHOSIS AND OTHER STORIES, Franz Kafka. Excellent new English translations of title story (considered by many critics Kafka's most perfect work), plus "The Judgment," "In the Penal Colony," "A Country Doctor," and "A Report to an Academy." Note. 96pp. 5³⁄₁₆ x 8¼. 0-486-29030-1

MICROSCOPIC ART FORMS FROM THE PLANT WORLD, R. Anheisser. From undulating curves to complex geometrics, a world of fascinating images abound in this classic, illustrated survey of microscopic plants. Features 400 detailed illustrations of nature's minute but magnificent handiwork. The accompanying CD-ROM includes all of the images in the book. 128pp. 9 x 9. 0-486-46013-4

A MIDSUMMER NIGHT'S DREAM, William Shakespeare. Among the most popular of Shakespeare's comedies, this enchanting play humorously celebrates the vagaries of love as it focuses upon the intertwined romances of several pairs of lovers. Explanatory footnotes. 80pp. 5³⁄₁₆ x 8¼. 0-486-27067-X

THE MONEY CHANGERS, Upton Sinclair. Originally published in 1908, this cautionary novel from the author of *The Jungle* explores corruption within the American system as a group of power brokers joins forces for personal gain, triggering a crash on Wall Street. 192pp. 5⅜ x 8½. 0-486-46917-4

THE MOST POPULAR HOMES OF THE TWENTIES, William A. Radford. With a New Introduction by Daniel D. Reiff. Based on a rare 1925 catalog, this architectural showcase features floor plans, construction details, and photos of 26 homes, plus articles on entrances, porches, garages, and more. 250 illustrations, 21 color plates. 176pp. 8⅜ x 11. 0-486-47028-8

MY 66 YEARS IN THE BIG LEAGUES, Connie Mack. With a New Introduction by Rich Westcott. A Founding Father of modern baseball, Mack holds the record for most wins — and losses — by a major league manager. Enhanced by 70 photographs, his warmhearted autobiography is populated by many legends of the game. 288pp. 5⅜ x 8½. 0-486-47184-5

NARRATIVE OF THE LIFE OF FREDERICK DOUGLASS, Frederick Douglass. Douglass's graphic depictions of slavery, harrowing escape to freedom, and life as a newspaper editor, eloquent orator, and impassioned abolitionist. 96pp. 5³⁄₁₆ x 8¼. 0-486-28499-9

THE NIGHTLESS CITY: Geisha and Courtesan Life in Old Tokyo, J. E. de Becker. This unsurpassed study from 100 years ago ventured into Tokyo's red-light district to survey geisha and courtesan life and offer meticulous descriptions of training, dress, social hierarchy, and erotic practices. 49 black-and-white illustrations; 2 maps. 496pp. 5⅜ x 8½. 0-486-45563-7

THE ODYSSEY, Homer. Excellent prose translation of ancient epic recounts adventures of the homeward-bound Odysseus. Fantastic cast of gods, giants, cannibals, sirens, other supernatural creatures — true classic of Western literature. 256pp. 5³⁄₁₆ x 8¼. 0-486-40654-7

OEDIPUS REX, Sophocles. Landmark of Western drama concerns the catastrophe that ensues when King Oedipus discovers he has inadvertently killed his father and married his mother. Masterly construction, dramatic irony. Explanatory footnotes. 64pp. 5³⁄₁₆ x 8¼. 0-486-26877-2

ONCE UPON A TIME: The Way America Was, Eric Sloane. Nostalgic text and drawings brim with gentle philosophies and descriptions of how we used to live — self-sufficiently — on the land, in homes, and among the things built by hand. 44 line illustrations. 64pp. 8⅜ x 11. 0-486-44411-2

ONE OF OURS, Willa Cather. The Pulitzer Prize–winning novel about a young Nebraskan looking for something to believe in. Alienated from his parents, rejected by his wife, he finds his destiny on the bloody battlefields of World War I. 352pp. 5³/₁₆ x 8¼. 0-486-45599-8

ORIGAMI YOU CAN USE: 27 Practical Projects, Rick Beech. Origami models can be more than decorative, and this unique volume shows how! The 27 practical projects include a CD case, frame, napkin ring, and dish. Easy instructions feature 400 two-color illustrations. 96pp. 8¼ x 11. 0-486-47057-1

OTHELLO, William Shakespeare. Towering tragedy tells the story of a Moorish general who earns the enmity of his ensign Iago when he passes him over for a promotion. Masterly portrait of an archvillain. Explanatory footnotes. 112pp. 5³/₁₆ x 8¼. 0-486-29097-2

PARADISE LOST, John Milton. Notes by John A. Himes. First published in 1667, *Paradise Lost* ranks among the greatest of English literature's epic poems. It's a sublime retelling of Adam and Eve's fall from grace and expulsion from Eden. Notes by John A. Himes. 480pp. 5³/₁₆ x 8¼. 0-486-44287-X

PASSING, Nella Larsen. Married to a successful physician and prominently ensconced in society, Irene Redfield leads a charmed existence — until a chance encounter with a childhood friend who has been "passing for white." 112pp. 5⅜ x 8½. 0-486-43713-2

PERSPECTIVE DRAWING FOR BEGINNERS, Len A. Doust. Doust carefully explains the roles of lines, boxes, and circles, and shows how visualizing shapes and forms can be used in accurate depictions of perspective. One of the most concise introductions available. 33 illustrations. 64pp. 5⅜ x 8½. 0-486-45149-6

PERSPECTIVE MADE EASY, Ernest R. Norling. Perspective is easy; yet, surprisingly few artists know the simple rules that make it so. Remedy that situation with this simple, step-by-step book, the first devoted entirely to the topic. 256 illustrations. 224pp. 5⅜ x 8½. 0-486-40473-0

THE PICTURE OF DORIAN GRAY, Oscar Wilde. Celebrated novel involves a handsome young Londoner who sinks into a life of depravity. His body retains perfect youth and vigor while his recent portrait reflects the ravages of his crime and sensuality. 176pp. 5³/₁₆ x 8¼. 0-486-27807-7

PRIDE AND PREJUDICE, Jane Austen. One of the most universally loved and admired English novels, an effervescent tale of rural romance transformed by Jane Austen's art into a witty, shrewdly observed satire of English country life. 272pp. 5³/₁₆ x 8¼. 0-486-28473-5

THE PRINCE, Niccolò Machiavelli. Classic, Renaissance-era guide to acquiring and maintaining political power. Today, nearly 500 years after it was written, this calculating prescription for autocratic rule continues to be much read and studied. 80pp. 5³/₁₆ x 8¼. 0-486-27274-5

QUICK SKETCHING, Carl Cheek. A perfect introduction to the technique of "quick sketching." Drawing upon an artist's immediate emotional responses, this is an extremely effective means of capturing the essential form and features of a subject. More than 100 black-and-white illustrations throughout. 48pp. 11 x 8¼. 0-486-46608-6

RANCH LIFE AND THE HUNTING TRAIL, Theodore Roosevelt. Illustrated by Frederic Remington. Beautifully illustrated by Remington, Roosevelt's celebration of the Old West recounts his adventures in the Dakota Badlands of the 1880s, from round-ups to Indian encounters to hunting bighorn sheep. 208pp. 6¼ x 9¼. 0-486-47340-6

THE RED BADGE OF COURAGE, Stephen Crane. Amid the nightmarish chaos of a Civil War battle, a young soldier discovers courage, humility, and, perhaps, wisdom. Uncanny re-creation of actual combat. Enduring landmark of American fiction. 112pp. 5³/₁₆ x 8¼. 0-486-26465-3

RELATIVITY SIMPLY EXPLAINED, Martin Gardner. One of the subject's clearest, most entertaining introductions offers lucid explanations of special and general theories of relativity, gravity, and spacetime, models of the universe, and more. 100 illustrations. 224pp. 5⅜ x 8½. 0-486-29315-7

REMBRANDT DRAWINGS: 116 Masterpieces in Original Color, Rembrandt van Rijn. This deluxe hardcover edition features drawings from throughout the Dutch master's prolific career. Informative captions accompany these beautifully reproduced landscapes, biblical vignettes, figure studies, animal sketches, and portraits. 128pp. 8⅜ x 11. 0-486-46149-1

THE ROAD NOT TAKEN AND OTHER POEMS, Robert Frost. A treasury of Frost's most expressive verse. In addition to the title poem: "An Old Man's Winter Night," "In the Home Stretch," "Meeting and Passing," "Putting in the Seed," many more. All complete and unabridged. 64pp. 5³/₁₆ x 8¼. 0-486-27550-7

ROMEO AND JULIET, William Shakespeare. Tragic tale of star-crossed lovers, feuding families and timeless passion contains some of Shakespeare's most beautiful and lyrical love poetry. Complete, unabridged text with explanatory footnotes. 96pp. 5³/₁₆ x 8¼. 0-486-27557-4

SANDITON AND THE WATSONS: Austen's Unfinished Novels, Jane Austen. Two tantalizing incomplete stories revisit Austen's customary milieu of courtship and venture into new territory, amid guests at a seaside resort. Both are worth reading for pleasure and study. 112pp. 5⅜ x 8½. 0-486-45793-1

THE SCARLET LETTER, Nathaniel Hawthorne. With stark power and emotional depth, Hawthorne's masterpiece explores sin, guilt, and redemption in a story of adultery in the early days of the Massachusetts Colony. 192pp. 5³/₁₆ x 8¼.
0-486-28048-9

THE SEASONS OF AMERICA PAST, Eric Sloane. Seventy-five illustrations depict cider mills and presses, sleds, pumps, stump-pulling equipment, plows, and other elements of America's rural heritage. A section of old recipes and household hints adds additional color. 160pp. 8⅜ x 11. 0-486-44220-9

SELECTED CANTERBURY TALES, Geoffrey Chaucer. Delightful collection includes the General Prologue plus three of the most popular tales: "The Knight's Tale," "The Miller's Prologue and Tale," and "The Wife of Bath's Prologue and Tale." In modern English. 144pp. 5³/₁₆ x 8¼. 0-486-28241-4

SELECTED POEMS, Emily Dickinson. Over 100 best-known, best-loved poems by one of America's foremost poets, reprinted from authoritative early editions. No comparable edition at this price. Index of first lines. 64pp. 5³/₁₆ x 8¼. 0-486-26466-1

SIDDHARTHA, Hermann Hesse. Classic novel that has inspired generations of seekers. Blending Eastern mysticism and psychoanalysis, Hesse presents a strikingly original view of man and culture and the arduous process of self-discovery, reconciliation, harmony, and peace. 112pp. 5³/₁₆ x 8¼. 0-486-40653-9

SKETCHING OUTDOORS, Leonard Richmond. This guide offers beginners step-by-step demonstrations of how to depict clouds, trees, buildings, and other outdoor sights. Explanations of a variety of techniques include shading and constructional drawing. 48pp. 11 x 8¼. 0-486-46922-0

SMALL HOUSES OF THE FORTIES: With Illustrations and Floor Plans, Harold E. Group. 56 floor plans and elevations of houses that originally cost less than $15,000 to build. Recommended by financial institutions of the era, they range from Colonials to Cape Cods. 144pp. 8⅜ x 11. 0-486-45598-X

SOME CHINESE GHOSTS, Lafcadio Hearn. Rooted in ancient Chinese legends, these richly atmospheric supernatural tales are recounted by an expert in Oriental lore. Their originality, power, and literary charm will captivate readers of all ages. 96pp. 5⅜ x 8½. 0-486-46306-0

SONGS FOR THE OPEN ROAD: Poems of Travel and Adventure, Edited by The American Poetry & Literacy Project. More than 80 poems by 50 American and British masters celebrate real and metaphorical journeys. Poems by Whitman, Byron, Millay, Sandburg, Langston Hughes, Emily Dickinson, Robert Frost, Shelley, Tennyson, Yeats, many others. Note. 80pp. 5$\frac{3}{16}$ x 8¼. 0-486-40646-6

SPOON RIVER ANTHOLOGY, Edgar Lee Masters. An American poetry classic, in which former citizens of a mythical midwestern town speak touchingly from the grave of the thwarted hopes and dreams of their lives. 144pp. 5$\frac{3}{16}$ x 8¼. 0-486-27275-3

STAR LORE: Myths, Legends, and Facts, William Tyler Olcott. Captivating retellings of the origins and histories of ancient star groups include Pegasus, Ursa Major, Pleiades, signs of the zodiac, and other constellations. "Classic." — *Sky & Telescope.* 58 illustrations. 544pp. 5⅜ x 8½. 0-486-43581-4

THE STRANGE CASE OF DR. JEKYLL AND MR. HYDE, Robert Louis Stevenson. This intriguing novel, both fantasy thriller and moral allegory, depicts the struggle of two opposing personalities — one essentially good, the other evil — for the soul of one man. 64pp. 5$\frac{3}{16}$ x 8¼. 0-486-26688-5

SURVIVAL HANDBOOK: The Official U.S. Army Guide, Department of the Army. This special edition of the Army field manual is geared toward civilians. An essential companion for campers and all lovers of the outdoors, it constitutes the most authoritative wilderness guide. 288pp. 5$\frac{3}{16}$ x 8¼. 0-486-46184-X

A TALE OF TWO CITIES, Charles Dickens. Against the backdrop of the French Revolution, Dickens unfolds his masterpiece of drama, adventure, and romance about a man falsely accused of treason. Excitement and derring-do in the shadow of the guillotine. 304pp. 5$\frac{3}{16}$ x 8¼. 0-486-40651-2

TEN PLAYS, Anton Chekhov. *The Sea Gull, Uncle Vanya, The Three Sisters, The Cherry Orchard,* and *Ivanov,* plus 5 one-act comedies: *The Anniversary, An Unwilling Martyr, The Wedding, The Bear,* and *The Proposal.* 336pp. 5$\frac{3}{16}$ x 8¼. 0-486-46560-8

THE FLYING INN, G. K. Chesterton. Hilarious romp in which pub owner Humphrey Hump and friend take to the road in a donkey cart filled with rum and cheese, inveighing against Prohibition and other "oppressive forms of modernity." 320pp. 5⅜ x 8½. 0-486-41910-X

THIRTY YEARS THAT SHOOK PHYSICS: The Story of Quantum Theory, George Gamow. Lucid, accessible introduction to the influential theory of energy and matter features careful explanations of Dirac's anti-particles, Bohr's model of the atom, and much more. Numerous drawings. 1966 edition. 240pp. 5⅜ x 8½. 0-486-24895-X

TREASURE ISLAND, Robert Louis Stevenson. Classic adventure story of a perilous sea journey, a mutiny led by the infamous Long John Silver, and a lethal scramble for buried treasure — seen through the eyes of cabin boy Jim Hawkins. 160pp. 5$\frac{3}{16}$ x 8¼. 0-486-27559-0

THE TRIAL, Franz Kafka. Translated by David Wyllie. From its gripping first sentence onward, this novel exemplifies the term "Kafkaesque." Its darkly humorous narrative recounts a bank clerk's entrapment in a bureaucratic maze, based on an undisclosed charge. 176pp. 5³⁄₁₆ x 8¼. 0-486-47061-X

THE TURN OF THE SCREW, Henry James. Gripping ghost story by great novelist depicts the sinister transformation of 2 innocent children into flagrant liars and hypocrites. An elegantly told tale of unspoken horror and psychological terror. 96pp. 5³⁄₁₆ x 8¼. 0-486-26684-2

UP FROM SLAVERY, Booker T. Washington. Washington (1856-1915) rose to become the most influential spokesman for African-Americans of his day. In this eloquently written book, he describes events in a remarkable life that began in bondage and culminated in worldwide recognition. 160pp. 5³⁄₁₆ x 8¼. 0-486-28738-6

VICTORIAN HOUSE DESIGNS IN AUTHENTIC FULL COLOR: 75 Plates from the "Scientific American – Architects and Builders Edition," 1885-1894, Edited by Blanche Cirker. Exquisitely detailed, exceptionally handsome designs for an enormous variety of attractive city dwellings, spacious suburban and country homes, charming "cottages" and other structures — all accompanied by perspective views and floor plans. 80pp. 9¼ x 12¼. 0-486-29438-2

VILLETTE, Charlotte Brontë. Acclaimed by Virginia Woolf as "Brontë's finest novel," this moving psychological study features a remarkably modern heroine who abandons her native England for a new life as a schoolteacher in Belgium. 480pp. 5³⁄₁₆ x 8¼. 0-486-45557-2

THE VOYAGE OUT, Virginia Woolf. A moving depiction of the thrills and confusion of youth, Woolf's acclaimed first novel traces a shipboard journey to South America for a captivating exploration of a woman's growing self-awareness. 288pp. 5³⁄₁₆ x 8¼. 0-486-45005-8

WALDEN; OR, LIFE IN THE WOODS, Henry David Thoreau. Accounts of Thoreau's daily life on the shores of Walden Pond outside Concord, Massachusetts, are interwoven with musings on the virtues of self-reliance and individual freedom, on society, government, and other topics. 224pp. 5³⁄₁₆ x 8¼. 0-486-28495-6

WILD PILGRIMAGE: A Novel in Woodcuts, Lynd Ward. Through startling engravings shaded in black and red, Ward wordlessly tells the story of a man trapped in an industrial world, struggling between the grim reality around him and the fantasies his imagination creates. 112pp. 6⅛ x 9¼. 0-486-46583-7

WILLY POGÁNY REDISCOVERED, Willy Pogány. Selected and Edited by Jeff A. Menges. More than 100 color and black-and-white Art Nouveau–style illustrations from fairy tales and adventure stories include scenes from Wagner's "Ring" cycle, *The Rime of the Ancient Mariner, Gulliver's Travels,* and *Faust.* 144pp. 8⅜ x 11. 0-486-47046-6

WOOLLY THOUGHTS: Unlock Your Creative Genius with Modular Knitting, Pat Ashforth and Steve Plummer. Here's the revolutionary way to knit — easy, fun, and foolproof! Beginners and experienced knitters need only master a single stitch to create their own designs with patchwork squares. More than 100 illustrations. 128pp. 6½ x 9¼. 0-486-46084-3

WUTHERING HEIGHTS, Emily Brontë. Somber tale of consuming passions and vengeance — played out amid the lonely English moors — recounts the turbulent and tempestuous love story of Cathy and Heathcliff. Poignant and compelling. 256pp. 5³⁄₁₆ x 8¼. 0-486-29256-8